The Land Tax of India

According to the Mohammedan Law
Translated from the Fatawa Alamgiri
with Explanatory Notes

Neil B. E. Baillie

Qadeem Press

Qadeem Press

Qadeem Press Edition
Breathing Life into Forgotten Pages
www.qadeempress.com

Originally Published by Smith, Elder, & Co. in 1873
Reprinted by Qadeem Press in 2025

Find our titles on your favourite online bookstore using the keyword 'Qadeem Press'

PREFACE

TO THE

FIRST EDITION.

The most important of the rights acquired by the East India Company, by cession or conquest, from its predecessors in the Government of India, is the *Khiraj* or Land Tax, which has existed in that country from early times, and was probably imposed upon it soon after its conquest by the Mohammedans. In Bengal, the right to this tax was conferred on the Company by an express grant from the Mogul Emperor, Shah Alum, under a Firman bearing date the 12th of August, 1765; and neither in that Presidency, nor in any other part of India, have the East India Company, or their local governors, ever pretended to any greater rights in respect of this particular tax, than belonged to the preceding governments, under the acknowledged law of the country. It has, therefore, always been considered a matter of importance to ascertain as correctly as possible the nature and limits of that tax, according to the Moohummudan Law, which was not only the general law of the country, but was more especially that which determined the rights of the Government and the people to each other. Enquirers on this subject have usually directed their investigations to the opinions prevailing among the people, and the practices of subordinate governors, rather than to the written records of the law. This may perhaps be accounted for by the fact, that the authorities of the Moohummudan Law are still in a great measure shut up in the Arabic language. The only original authority on the Law of the *Khiraj*, hitherto accessible to the mere English reader, is the rather confused account of it which is contained in Mr. Hamilton's translation of the *Hidayah*. Unless perused with care, and some previous knowledge of the subject, that account may in some respects mislead the reader, and it is scarcely intelligible without the aid of commentaries on the work, that are still to be found only in the Arabic language. For this reason, in continuing my extracts from the Futawa Alumgeeree, I have selected this part of the law as not only of great importance in itself, but also as that which, after Sale, is perhaps involved in the greatest obscurity, and most requires elucidation.

The following pages contain all that I have been able to find in the six volumes of the Futawa Alumgeeree, having a direct bearing on the *Khiraj* or Land Tax. Their extent bears no proportion to the amount of labour which has been expended in compiling them, or in acquiring the knowledge necessary to their proper explanation. The explanation is contained partly in an Introduction, and partly in the Notes. In the former I have endeavoured to deduce the leading principles of the Law, and to apply them to the present system of Land Revenue. The latter have been derived from other parts of the Futawa Alumgeeree, and from the Hidayah and two of its Commentaries, the Kifayah and Inayah. In the Introductory Essay, the Shuraya-ool-Islam, a Treatise on the Sheea doctrines, is also occasionally referred to.[1] All these works, which are in Arabic, have been printed at Calcutta, under the authority of the Committee of Public Instruction. The Hidayah and Kifayah are printed together, and the combined work is referred to under the double or

[1] Omitted in the present Essay.

single name, as the reference is to both text and comment, or to one or the other of them. When the Hidayah is cited, the Translation by Mr. Hamilton is usually referred to at the same time, the latter as the Hedaya, the word being so spelled in the title of the Translation, while the original is cited as the Hidayah, according to the spelling in the English title-page of the printed edition. For an account of the original compilation of the Futawa Alumgeeree, and the authorities of the Moohummudan Law, I beg leave to refer the reader to the Preliminary Remarks and Introduction to my book on the Moohummudan Law of Sale.

It is now necessary to say a few words of the contents of this very brief volume. The *Khiraj* is closely connected in origin with another tax or impost on the produce of land, called the *Ooshr* or tithe, and they are commonly treated of under one head, by the writers on the Moohummudan Law. The *Ooshr*, however, is a branch of a more general impost, called the *Zukat*, which is applicable to charitable purposes. The first chapter of the following selections treats of the *Ooshr* and *Khiraj* conjointly. In the second, the *Ooshr* is considered with reference to its nature as the *Zukat* on fruits and crops. The third contains some extracts relating to the original imposition of the *Ooshr* and *Khiraj* upon different lands. These two imposts are taxes on the productive energies of the soil; but some things below its surface are liable to the deduction of a fifth. Accordingly, the fourth chapter treats of the *Khooms*, or fifth on metals and buried treasures. It is the proprietor of the land who is liable for the *Ooshr* and *Khiraj*, and in most cases for the *Khooms*. The question of proprietorship in the land is thus of great collateral importance. The fifth chapter shows how the proprietorship of waste land is acquired by bringing it into cultivation. But a proprietor is not always in possession of his own land, and the possessor of it may sometimes be confounded with him. The last chapter, therefore, treats of a peculiar contract called *Moozâraüt*, by which the relations of proprietor and possessor, or landlord and tenant as they would be called by us, have been commonly regulated in Mohammedan countries.

An Appendix is added, containing some documents which are referred to in the Introductory Essay. One of these is worthy of more particular notice. It is a copy of the translation of a Firman, addressed by the Emperor Aurungzebe, apparently by way of circular, to the Dewans of his different provinces; and is of value, not only as showing the state of the *Khiraj*, at a time when the Mohammedan power was in its strength, but also as demonstrating that the Digest of the Law, which was prepared by this Emperor's command, was practically carried into effect, in one important department, by his own express authority. This document is considered to be of so much importance in the last point of view, that notes have been added to it, referring to the corresponding parts in the text.

It is proper to add, that this work, like its predecessor, on the Moohummudan Law of Sale, is published at the expense of the East India Company. This is no pledge for its accuracy, nor any sanction for the opinions expressed in the Introductory Essay. For these, the writer alone is responsible. But he hopes that he may refer to this renewed instance of the liberality of the Court of Directors, as an earnest of the value which it continues to attach to expositions of the Moohummudan Law. He takes this opportunity of repeating his acknowledgments to all the members of the Court, and begs leave, as a mark of his respect, to inscribe a work on which their patronage has bestowed some importance, to their present enlightened Chairman, Sir JAMES WEIR HOGG, Baronet.

GLOUCESTER TERRACE, HYDE PARK,
31*st March*, 1853.

ADVERTISEMENT

TO THE

SECOND EDITION.

In the former edition of the Introductory Essay, I adopted the theory of the Bengal Regulations with respect to the relative rights of the Zemindars and Ryots. A further examination of the authorities led me to doubt the correctness of that theory; and my doubts have been confirmed by the light incidentally cast upon the subject by the late Sir Henry Elliott's valuable collection of the Native Historians of India. Much of the Essay that had been adapted to views that I am now satisfied are erroneous has thus become superfluous; and I have thought that by recasting the whole and omitting everything that was merely speculative, the work might be made practically more useful. What is now presented to the reader is in some respects rather a new essay than a second edition of the old one. It is divided into four parts. The first contains an account of the history and nature of the *Khiraj* or Mohammedan Land Tax; the second, its application to British India, including its effect on the tenure of land; the third, the changes that have taken place in these tenures since the transfer of the Dewany or Civil Government of Bengal, Behar, and Orissa to the East India Company; and the fourth, the *Lakhiraj* tenures, or such as are exempt from the *Khiraj*.

The following abbreviations are used in the references to authorities:—

Fut. Al. for Futawa Alumgeeree.

Maverdy for the Uhkam Sultaneeah of that author.

Ay. Akb. for the Ayeen Akbery. Mr. Gladwin's Translation. Q[to] edition.

Elliott for the History of India as told by its own Historians, by the late Sir H. Elliott.

Ap. F. R. for the Appendix to the Fifth Report from the Select Committee on the affairs of the East India Company.

Digest for Digest of Moohummudan Law. N. B. E. Baillie.

For mode of referring to the Hidayah see Preface, p. iii.

By Regulations those of the Government of Bengal are meant where not otherwise specified.

The references within parentheses in the text are to the body of the work, which is the same as in the first edition.

CONTENTS

OF

THE INTRODUCTORY ESSAY.

CONTENTS

OF

THE LAND TAX OF INDIA.

INTRODUCTORY ESSAY.

THERE are two duties or imposts, to one or other of which the cultivated land in Mohammedan countries, or its produce, is generally liable. One of these is the *Ooshr* or tithe, and land subject to it is called *Ooshree*; the other is the *Khiraj* or tribute, and the land subject to it is called *Khirajee*. *Ooshr*, in the language of the law, is the *Zukat* or poor-rate on the fruits of the earth. *Khiraj*, in the same language, is a peculiar rate or duty imposed upon the lands of conquered countries whose inhabitants have been left free to the exercise of their own religion. *Ooshr* is due only on the actual produce of the soil. *Khiraj* is due on productive land, whether it yield any produce or not. *Khiraj* is thus more onerous than *Ooshr*, and falls more properly on infidels or unbelievers in the Mussulman religion; while *Ooshr*, for the opposite reason, is more appropriate to Mooslims.[1] Mooslims, moreover, cannot be taxed without their own consent; and *Khiraj*, therefore, cannot be imposed on their lands except under peculiar circumstances. *Ooshr* may be imposed under any circumstances, because, being a religious duty, their consent is implied. *Ooshr*, again, cannot be received from an infidel; for it involves an act of piety of which he is deemed to be incapable. There is no objection, however, to the receipt of *Khiraj* from a Mooslim. The land of the former, therefore, is necessarily subject to *Khiraj*; while that of the latter may be subject either to *Ooshr* or

Ooshr and *Khiraj*.

[1] *Hidayah* and *Kifayah*, vol. ii. p. 775.

Khiraj. No land can be subject to both *Ooshr* and *Khiraj* at the same time.[1]

How first imposed upon the land of conquered countries.

The circumstances under which the land of Mohammedan countries became originally subject to *Ooshr* or *Khiraj* are detailed in the third chapter of the following selections. The law on the subject may be briefly summed up as follows :—It is founded on a supposed obligation of all mankind to embrace what is called the true religion, or to submit to the true 'Believers,' and the counter obligation of the true believers to war upon all men to the last extremity, until they adopt one or other of these alternatives. Before commencing a war for this purpose, it is the duty of the *Imam*, or head of the Mooslim community, to invite the inhabitants of the country which he is about to invade, to embrace the true religion; and without this formality the war is unlawful. If they accept the invitation, they are to be treated in all respects like other Mooslims, and the *Ooshr*, as a matter of course, is imposed on their lands. If they reject the invitation, they are next to be called on to submit to the *Juzyut*, or capitation tax, and become subjects of the Mooslim power. If they accept these terms, they are admitted to the condition of *Zimmees* or subjects, and are left free to the profession of their own religion; but the *Khiraj* is imposed upon their lands. The idolaters of Arabia were excepted from this indulgence, and were called upon absolutely to embrace the faith, with the only alternative of the sword for their men, and slavery for their women and children. If the people to whom the call to *Islam* or the *Juzyut* is addressed reject both the alternatives, they are to be warred upon to the last extremity, and, if conquered, the whole of their property passes to the conquerors, without any distinction between what is moveable and what is immoveable, or between what belongs to the State and what to private individuals. The moveable property is plunder, without

[1] According to Shafei, the leader of another of the Soonnee sects, when a Mooslim cultivates *Khirajee* land, the produce is subject to *Ooshr* as well as to the *Khiraj*.—Maverdy, pp. 205–6.

any difference of opinion among Soonnees, and ought to be divided among the soldiers of the conquering army. According to Shafei, the land also is plunder, and should in like manner be divided among the soldiers. According to Malik, it becomes *wukf*, or an appropriation for the general benefit of Mussulmans. According to Aboo Huneefa, the Imam, or head of the Mussulman community, has an option, and may divide the land among the soldiers, or bestow it on the people of the country, even though they should persist in rejecting the true religion, or he may reserve it in the manner of a *wukf*, for the purposes of war.[1] If he adopts the first alternative, *Ooshr*, or tithe is to be imposed upon the land, unless it is connected with what is called *Khiraj* water; while if he should bestow the land upon the conquered people, the *Khiraj* is to be imposed upon it. The reason assigned for this[2] is that, being due, whether the land is cultivated or not, it is burdensome, and, being in the nature of a punishment, is thought to be more appropriate than *Ooshr* to their condition as infidels. According to one authority (p. 2), connection with *Khiraj* water is a condition of the imposition of *Khiraj*, even when land is bestowed on the original inhabitants without their embracing the faith of Islam; and this view is supported to some extent by a passage in Mr. Hamilton's translation of the *Hidayah*.[3] But the translation is not borne out by the printed original,[4] and the author of the *Hidayah* himself asserts positively[5] that the conquered land in the supposed case is *ipso facto Khirajee*, though he adverts to a somewhat different opinion in the *Jama Sagheer*. Other authorities (p. 35) support the assertion of the author of the *Hidayah*, averring positively that, when the Imam grants their lives and freedom together with their property to the inhabitants of the conquered country, he may impose the *Khiraj* on their lands whether the water be *Ooshree* or *Khirajee*. And this conclusion is confirmed by the consideration

[1] *Fut. Al.* vol. ii. p. 291. [2] *Hidayah* and *Kifayah*, vol. ii. p. 775. [3] Vol. ii. p. 206. [4] Vol. ii. p. 775. [5] *Ibid.*

that otherwise unbelievers would have the land on a more favourable condition than Mooslims, as *Ooshr* cannot be received from infidels. Reason, as well as the weight of authority, is thus in favour of religion as being the leading principle for determining the liability of land to *Ooshr* or *Khiraj*. When lands are conferred on persons who are not of the Musulman faith, *Khiraj* is the proper duty, without reference to any distinction of waters; when it is conferred on Mooslims, *Ooshr* is the proper duty; and it is only when the land is connected with *Khiraj* water that the *Khiraj* can be imposed upon it.

The same rules are applicable generally to waste lands (pp. 3 and 48) when first brought into cultivation. It is, therefore, still of some importance to endeavour to ascertain exactly what waters are *Ooshr* water and what are *Khiraj*.

Ooshr and Khiraj water.

The authorities on the subject are long subsequent to the first imposition of the *Khiraj*, and must therefore be understood as indicating the waters that were held to be *Ooshr* and *Khiraj* waters in the time of the writers rather than such as were originally so. The first authority on the subject in the following selections is an extract from the *Shurih-Tahavee* (p. 2), where, referring to what produce of land is subject to *Ooshr*, it is said, that 'it makes no difference whether the land be watered by rain from the heavens or by running water;' thus indicating that there is some difference between waters derived from these respective sources.

Further on we have extracts from the *Moheet* and the *Kafee* (p. 28), in which *Ooshr* and *Khiraj* waters are distinctly opposed to each other, and the former is said to be the water of wells and fountains in *Ooshree* land, together with rain and the waters of great seas; while the latter is said to be the water of wells and fountains in *Khirajee* land, together with the water of the Persian canals and the great rivers Syhoon, Tigris, and Euphrates. Leaving the waters of wells and fountains out of consideration on both sides for the present, we have only rain and the water of great seas as *Ooshr* water on the one side, with the Persian canals and the waters of the Syhoon, Tigris, and

Euphrates as *Khiraj* water on the other. By seas are to be understood any large bodies of water, and the term is qualified in the *Hidayah*[1] by the words 'which are not under the power of any one.' The same thing may manifestly be predicated of rain, and this is apparently the point in which rain and the water of great seas or lakes agree with each other, and both are distinguished from the canals and great rivers particularly mentioned. With regard to the rivers, there was a difference of opinion among the Hanifite doctors. Moohummud thought that they are not under the power of anyone, since no one can protect their waters so as to prevent their use by others; that therefore their waters are *Ooshr* waters. Aboo Huneefa and Aboo Yoosuf, on the other hand, held them to be *Khiraj* waters. The reason of Aboo Huneefa's opinion is not given, but Aboo Yoosuf's was founded on the consideration that bridges of boats being cast across their streams they may be said to be brought under the power of some one. Without having recourse to the reason assigned by Aboo Yoosuf, it may, I think, be fairly assumed that the waters as well as the land of a country are generally under the power of its inhabitants or their rulers, and therefore pass by conquest over them to their conquerors. They may, accordingly, like the land, be divided by the Imam among his soldiers, or restored to the original inhabitants. Wells and fountains can hardly be separated from the lands in which they are situated, and would naturally become *Ooshr* or *Khiraj* water, according as the *Ooshr* or *Khiraj* were imposed on the land. Other waters may be comprehended generally under the head of running waters or rivers. Of these the smaller rivers might be distributed among classes of persons or individuals, pretty much in the same way as the land, and their waters might thus become *Ooshr* or *Khiraj* water, according as the land through which they passed were made the one or the other. The greater rivers, on the other hand, passing through many countries, could

[1] Translation, vol. i. p. 51.

not be so distributed, and would therefore always remain under the control of the Imam. This we are told was actually the case. Rivers are said to be of three kinds (p. 49)—1st. Great or public rivers; 2nd. General rivers; and 3rd. Private rivers. Of these the two last, though distinguished from each other in some respects, agree in this, that they have both entered into division; while the first class, of which the three rivers already mentioned, together with the Jyhoon and Nile, are given as types, have never been divided. They remain, therefore, under the power of the Imam for the general benefit of the Mussulman community; and on him is imposed the duty of keeping their channels clear. For this purpose he may employ the funds of the *Khiraj* department of the public treasury, or, if there be none, even compel the people to work (p. 49). It may therefore be assumed that he must have some power over the use of their waters. The only way in which this seems to have been exercised in the olden times was by imposing the *Khiraj* on land fructified by them. In later times duties may have been imposed upon merchandise passing through their channels, and this may possibly be the origin of the tolls which are still levied at some places on the great rivers of India. Water being the great fructifying element of land in countries where heat, the other element, is usually in excess, the waters of the great rivers would naturally be termed *Khiraj* waters, as the source from which the *Khiraj* was ultimately derived; while rain and the water of the great seas or lakes would as naturally be termed *Ooshr* water, as the source from which the *Ooshr* was ultimately derived. This seems to have been the reason for applying the terms *Ooshree* and *Khirajee* to water as well as to land; for the termination *ee* in both words signifies nothing more than relation generally.

Countries that are *Khirajee*.

The Sowad of Irak, on which Omar imposed the *Khiraj* when he restored the lands to the original inhabitants, was watered by the Persian canals. Syria, on which he also imposed it, and Egypt, on which it was imposed by Amroo Ebn-al-Aas, are both watered by great or public rivers. In none of these cases does it appear that any distinction was made on account of the religion of the persons on whom the land was bestowed. On Arabia, again, of which only a very small part, if any, can be said to be within the influence of a great or public river, the *Khiraj* was never imposed by the Prophet or any of his successors, though a part of the land was left in the possession of a Christian tribe called the Beni Toghlib. The whole of Arabia, therefore, is *Ooshree*. But upon the lands of the Tooghlibees a double *Ooshr* was imposed; and to meet the difficulty of the *Ooshr* not being properly receivable from any but Mooslims, this *Ooshr* is carried to the *Khiraj* department of the public treasury, where it is applied to the same purpose as the *Khiraj*. The double *Ooshr* having been imposed on the *Tooghlibees* under a special composition, which is termed *Sooluh*, the land so subjected to the double *Ooshr* has been termed Sooluhee; and the lands of the whole Mohammedan world have thus come to be sometimes described as of three kinds, *Ooshree*, *Khirajee*, and *Sooluhee*. Corresponding with these three descriptions of land are three classes of persons, all of whom are termed *Maliks*, or proprietors, viz., Mooslims; *Zimmees*, or infidel subjects in general; and *Tooghlibees*, or persons belonging to the tribe of *Tooghlib*.[1]

Others that are *Ooshree*.

Ooshree land may become *Khirajee*.

If land is purchased from a Tooghlibee by a Zimmee, it remains subject to the double *Ooshr*, according to all opinions. So also, according to Moohummud, if it is purchased by a Mooslim, or the Tooghlibee himself is converted to the faith; and even if *Ooshree* land be transferred from a Mooslim to a *Zimmee*, or a *Tooghlibee*, it remains, according to Moohummud, subject to *Ooshr* as before, the character originally impressed upon it being indelible in his opinion. According to Aboo Yoosuf, if a Tooghlibee transfer his land to a Mooslim, the latter is liable only for a single *Ooshr*; while if a Mooslim sell his *Ooshree* land to a *Zimmee*, the purchaser becomes liable

[1] *Kifayah*, vol. i. p. 535. And see *Ay. Akb.* vol. i. p. 349.

to a double *Ooshr*; the land, in Aboo Yoosuf's opinion, changing its character with the religion of its owner. Aboo Huneefa agreed with Moohummud with regard to the transfer of Tooghlibee land to a Mooslim, but differed from him as to *Ooshree* land, which, when transferred to a *Zimmee*, and taken possession of by him, loses its character, according to Aboo Huneefa, and becomes *Khirajee*. If the land is taken by another Mooslim under a claim of pre-emption, or is returned to the seller on account of a defect, it becomes again liable to *Ooshr*, as before. But these are the only instances mentioned of a return to its original character; and it may therefore be presumed that, the land having become *Khirajee*, would, in the opinion of Aboo Huneefa, remain so though subsequently transferred to a Mooslim. When the three doctors differ, the opinion of Aboo Huneefa is generally received as law, and, accordingly, though the *Hidayah* is quoted as the authority, only so much of it as contains his opinion is given on this point in the *Futawa Alumgeeree* (p. 27).

Khirajee land maintains its character under all changes of property.

It is only *Ooshree* and *Sooluhee* lands that are thus liable to mutations of character upon transfer to persons of different religions. The character of *Khirajee* land remains unchanged in every mutation of property, according to the three doctors; and this, with the changes to which *Ooshree* land is liable according to the prevailing opinion, will account for the small quantity of *Ooshree* land which may now be found in some countries that have been long subject to Mohammedan rule. In India, the *Ooshree* character seems to be entirely lost, and the name is I believe hardly known.

Waste land when brought into cultivation, how subjected to *Ooshr* or *Khiraj*.

Waste land when brought into cultivation by a Mooslim, is, according to Aboo Yoosuf, *Ooshree* if contiguous to *Ooshree* land, and *Khirajee* if contiguous to *Khirajee* land; but, according to Moohummud, it is the one or the other according to the nature of the water by means of which it has been reclaimed. When brought into cultivation by a *Zimmee*, it is *Khirajee* under all circumstances and without any difference of opinion (p. 48).

Khiraj,

Having now determined the conditions under which

land is subject to *Ooshr* or *Khiraj* in Mohammedan countries, and shown the tendency of *Ooshree* land ultimately to become *Khirajee*, let us attend a little more closely to the special character of the *Khiraj*, with a view to ascertain if we can the relative rights in the land of the parties to and by whom it is payable.

Its special character.

Existed in the Sowad before the conquest.

A tax of the same nature as the *Khiraj* existed in the Sowad of Irak in the time of its Persian rulers. It was originally levied by a division of the produce between the sovereign and the cultivator. But that mode of levying the tax being deemed oppressive by Cobad, he caused the land to be measured, and imposed a rate of a *kufeez* in grain and a *dirhem* in money upon each *jureeb* of it. Some say that this was done by his more celebrated son Nowshirvan, and it is probable that the arrangement commenced by the father was completed by the son. A *kufeez* was held to be of the value of three *dirhems*, so that the whole rate thus imposed upon the land was equivalent to four *dirhems* on every *jureeb*. Up to this time there seems to have been no legal limit to the sovereign's demand, but it is said of the Khoosroes, or Persian sovereigns, by Mohammedan writers (p. 19) that, when calamity overtook the crop of the cultivator they used to indemnify him for his seed and maintenance, saying: 'The *Moozarea* is our partner in profit, how then shall we not share with him in loss?' From this it would seem that, in the opinion of these writers, a co-partnership in the produce subsisted between the sovereign and the cultivator, like that which was afterwards known in the Mohammedan law under the name of *Moozâraŭt*. That contract is similar to the metayer system of Europe; and, under both systems, the cultivator is no more than a tenant holding under another who is the proprietor of the soil. According to that analogy, the rulers of the Sowad were originally the proprietors of the land. But the analogy fails after the conversion of their share in the produce to a fixed rate on every *jureeb* of the land; for the reservation under a contract of *Moozârŭnt* of a fixed quantity, instead of a share in the produce, vitiates that contract (p. 54). The cultivators would, therefore, cease to be *Moozareas* after the settlement by Cobad, and would, in the view of the Mohammedan lawyers, become proprietors, if only for want of any other category in which to place them.

Persian tax adopted by Omar with some variations.

The tax to which the land of the Sowad was found to be subjected at the time of the Mussulman conquest was generally adopted by Omar, but increased for some kinds of produce, which were supposed to require a less degree of labour to bring them to maturity. Thus, the rate imposed upon a *Jureeb*, or square of sixty *zira* of grain, was, as already observed, equivalent in value to four *dirhems*. On the same extent of vegetables or plants whose roots remain in the ground for several years, the rate imposed was five *dirhems* in money; and on a similar quantity of land planted with vines and date trees, which were calculated to endure for many years, the rate imposed was ten *dirhems*. It does not appear, that at the time when the assessment was made, there were any other kinds of produce in the Sowad than such as fell under one or other of the three descriptions above mentioned. But saffron and cotton are specified in the *Hidayah* and other authorities as not being included; and gardens or pleasure-grounds, where the trees are too widely dispersed to allow of their being classed with vineyards or date orchards, are also noticed as being different from any of the descriptions mentioned. In cases of this kind, for which the example of Omar afforded no precedent, a *Khiraj* was afterwards imposed as the occasion arose, which was some proportionate share of the whole produce.

Khiraj divided into two kinds, *Mookasumah* and *Wuzeefa.*

The *Khiraj* came thus to be divided into two kinds, *Mookasumah* and *Wuzeefa*. The former is a share of the produce, as a fifth, a sixth, or the like, and depends on the actual crop or issue from the land, not on the kind of crop which it is capable of bearing; in so much that, like *Ooshr*, it is not due when the land, though capable, is allowed to lie idle. The latter, or *Wuzeefa*, is 'something in obligation,' that is, a personal liability on account of a definite portion of land, and is dependent on the return that the land is capable of yielding. It is, therefore due so long as the land retains its capability, whether it be cultivated or not. It has thus that quality which is supposed to render *Khiraj* more appropriate than *Ooshr* to the lands of unbelievers, and we might therefore reasonably infer that, when the lands of a conquered country are restored to the original inhabitants, without requiring their adoption of the faith of Islam, it is the *Wuzeefa*, and not the *Mookasumah*, that would be imposed upon them. We are not left to conjecture upon this point; for in the only undoubted examples we have of the formal imposition of *Khiraj* on the land of any conquered country, viz., that of Omar in the cases of the Sowad, Syria and Egypt, there is no doubt that the *Khiraj* was *Wuzeefa*. Again, when *Ooshree* land is transferred from a Mooslim to a Zimmee, and becomes liable to *Khiraj*, as already mentioned, it is the same quality peculiar to the *Wuzeefa*, of being due whether the land is cultivated or not, that has been assigned as the reason for the change of the impost;[1] and it is therefore the *Wuzeefa* which must be imposed on the land in such circumstances. Further, when waste land is brought into cultivation and becomes liable to *Khiraj*, it is the *Wuzeefa* which is to be imposed upon it, for it is expressly said that a liability to *Wuzeefa* is one of the effects or consequences that result from the reclaiming of waste (p. 48). These are the only cases in which we can predicate with any certainty that the *Khiraj* has ever been imposed upon the land of a conquered country; and in all of them it is evident that, in the opinion of the Hanifite doctors, the establishment of a right of property in the land in favour of some one is a necessary preliminary to the imposition of the *Khiraj*. In the two first cases the establishment of the right, as we have seen, is by positive grant from the conquerors, and in the last by the act of reclamation from waste, as will be shown hereafter.[2] Accordingly, the lands of the Sowad on which *Khiraj* was im-

[1] *Hedaya*, vol. i. p. 536.

[2] Post. p. xxvi.

posed for the first time, are expressly said to be "the property of the inhabitants, who may lawfully sell or otherwise dispose of them;"[1] and generally, by Hanifite writers, the *Khiraj* is said to be due by the proprietors of the land, as if there must in all cases be a proprietor of *Khirajee* land, distinct from the party to whom the *Khiraj* is payable. It is true that this is said of the *Khiraj* generally, but there is no personal responsibility in the case of *Mookasumah*, and it must therefore be of the *Wuzeefa* that the writers are speaking. Moreover, there is only the doubtful instance of Kheiber on record, in which it seems that anything like a *Mookasumah Khiraj* was ever formally imposed upon any land. Of this case two accounts are given in the *Hidayah*. In one it is said that the Prophet divided the lands among his followers.[2] In the other that he left the lands in the possession of the inhabitants on condition of their giving him half the produce. This is the view that was taken of the case both by Aboo Huneefa and his two disciples; but while he refers to the case as an example of *Mookasumah Khiraj*, they insist that it was one of *Mozâraüt*. They all, however, seem to have agreed that whatever was done was by way of special composition, which agrees with what we are told by the historians, that it was not till after a long and valiant resistance, that the people of Kheiber surrendered upon the terms referred to.[4] In no sense, therefore, does the case form a precedent for the disposal of lands acquired by mere force of arms. The conclusion, then, to which I have come on the whole matter is, that wherever we find land subject to a *Wuzeefa Khiraj* in a country acquired by force of arms, there, both by reason and precedent, we ought to infer that the land is the property of the persons by whom the *Khiraj* is rendered or paid; but that wherever, on the other hand, the *Khiraj* is *Mookasumah*, we have neither reason nor precedent for the same inference,

Land subject to *Wuzeefa* is the property of parties by whom it is payable.

1 *Hedaya*, vol. ii. p. 205.
2 P. 159.
3 *Ibid.* vol. iv. p. 39.
4 *Mod. Un. History*, vol. i. p. 113.

and ought rather to conclude, if only for want of evidence to the contrary, that the conquerors have never parted with the rights acquired by conquest, and that the land therefore is the property of the sovereign as representative of the Imam, or Head of the Mussulman community.

Rate of the *Wuzeefa* when first imposed cannot exceed that of Omar, though it may be less.

The rates of the *Wuzeefa* are restricted to those established by Omar. No higher rate can, according to the prevailing opinion among the Hanifites, be lawfully imposed on any land in the first instance by any of his successors. But there is no doubt that the rate may be less if the land is unable to bear one so high. Omar himself is said to have imposed lower rates upon Syria. Thus, instead of a uniform rate of a *kufeez* and a *dirhem* for every *jureeb* of land fit for sowing, he is said to have restricted that rate to land fit for wheat, and to have imposed only two *dirhems* on the *jureeb* of land fit only for barley. So also, instead of a uniform rate of ten *dirhems* for a *jureeb* of orchards, he reduced the rate to eight *dirhems* for date trees, and to six for sugar-cane. So that he seems to have made the capability of the land his standard of rating in all cases; and, accordingly, the rule which has been deduced from his example, for all cases in which he has left no positive precedent, is to impose such rates as the land may be supposed to be capable of bearing with reference to its natural fertility, the kind of crops commonly grown upon it, and its facilities in respect of water—circumstances in which some lands differ materially from others.[1] No land is supposed to be capable of bearing a rate exceeding half of its produce. That, therefore, is said to be the extreme of capability; and any *Wuzeefa* in excess of it would be unlawful.

Rate of *Mookasumah* cannot exceed half the produce.

The same rule is applicable to the imposition of the *Mookasumah*, which may be any share of the produce not exceeding a half; the exact proportion being left to the Imam to fix as he may think proper (p. 7).

[1] Maverdy, p. 257. Considerations of this kind seem to have influenced Akbar in his assessment of India. He also kept in view the neighbourhood of cities.—*Ay. Akb.* vol. i. p. 347.

So far as to the original imposition of the *Khiraj*. If, by reason of a falling-off of the crop, the land should be unable to bear the rates imposed upon it, they may be lawfully reduced according to all opinions (p. 6); whether an addition can be made to the rates when, by reason of an abundant crop, the land is able to bear it, is liable to doubts. According to Moohummud, the addition is lawful, but not so according to Aboo Yoosuf, and the author of the *Hidayah* seems to favour his opinion.[1] But the compilers of the *Futawa Alumgeeree* receive the doctrine with some qualification. They say that, if the rates were originally imposed by Omar himself, or by an Imam acting in express accordance with his example, it would not be competent to him to make any addition to them without the consent of the people, even though the land were able to bear the addition. Still, if he should make the addition, or convert a *Wuzeefa* to a *Mookasumah*, or *vice versa*, and his successor should approve of the act, he may lawfully give currency to it, provided that the land had been originally subdued by force of arms, and then bestowed upon the people. But if the people had peaceably submitted before the grant was made to them, the act of the preceding ruler should be cancelled. In all cases, therefore, it would seem that, according to the last quoted authority, the *Khiraj* of a conquered country may be increased or varied from one kind to the other at the will of the sovereign, provided that the land is able to bear it, and that it is never raised above a half of the produce.

Sovereign entitled to receive the *Khiraj*.

Be that as it may, there is no doubt that the sovereign is in all cases entitled to receive the *Khiraj*, and we have now to enquire what remedies he has for its recovery.

Remedies for its recovery.

The *Wuzeefa* being a personal liability of the owner of the land, he may be sued for it as for an ordinary debt, and even imprisoned in case of non-payment. There is no such remedy in the case of the *Mookasumah*, but the occupant of the land has no right to appropriate any part of the produce to his own use, until the proportion appli-

[1] *Hedaya*, vol. ii. p. 208.

cable to the *Khiraj* has first been deducted from it, and until that is done the sovereign has a lien on the whole crop, and may prevent any part of it from being removed (p. 22). In no case has he any right to deprive the proprietors of their lands and transfer them in property to another, even though the land should be allowed to lie idle for want of means to cultivate it, or though it should be abandoned altogether. The proper course to be pursued in such circumstances is first to let the land to an ordinary tenant, or if none can be found willing to take it on hire, then to deliver it to some one in *Moozâraŭt*, and to deduct the *Khiraj* from the rent, or share in the produce, as the case may be, reserving the remainder for the proprietor. Should no person be found willing to take the land on hire or in *Moozâraŭt*, it may then be delivered to anyone willing to abide on it for the mere *Khiraj*; and it is only in the extreme case when all other methods have failed, that the land may be sold and the *Khiraj* be deducted out of the price, the remainder, if any, being handed over to the proprietor, or kept for him if he should happen to return (p. 14).

General purposes and persons on whom the *Khiraj* may be expended.

The purposes to which the *Khiraj* is to be applied may be described generally as works and services for the benefit of the Mussulman community; and the persons upon whom it may be expended, such as soldiers, governors and their assistants, *kazees*, *mooftees* and police, and the students and teachers of learning, are termed *Ahl* or people of *Khiraj*. When the owner of *Khirajee* land belongs to any of these classes, the ruler may apply to him the *Khiraj* of his own land, that is, leave it with him uncalled for. On this principle it is expressly said that a disposal of the *Khiraj* in favour of *kazees* and lawyers would be lawful (p. 11). It may perhaps be inferred that what the sovereign may do in favour of the owner of the land, he may also do in favour of one who is not the owner; that is, authorise such a person, being duly qualified, to receive and appropriate for his own benefit the *Khiraj* of any particular land, though it may happen to be the property of others. Whatever may be done in this way is called an *Iktaa*, which means literally a cutting off, as if the exercise of the sovereign's power in the particular instance were a separation of something from a general fund belonging to the community.

Iktaa, or a pecial application of the *Khiraj*.

The authority before quoted does not seem to go beyond the *Khiraj* of one year, but we are informed by Maverdy [1] that *Iktaas* for several years, ten for instance, are lawful, provided that the persons on whom they are bestowed are in the pay of the State, having a fixed allowance entered on the public registers. Soldiers are particularly mentioned as having special claims to *Iktaas*, which in this case are only a compensation for the lives which they devote to the public service. When the *Khiraj* is thus granted for a term of years, as ten for instance, and the grantee dies before its expiration, the grant is annulled on the instant, and the *Khiraj* reverts to the public treasury.[2] But a question may arise as to its disposal in the event of the grantee's falling sick during the term, and remaining ill till its expiration, so as to be incapable of performing the service for which it was granted. On this point there is a division of opinion, some thinking that the grant should be allowed to continue till the expiration of the term, others that it should be annulled, as in the case of the death of the grantee.[3]

If the grant be for life there is a difference of opinion as to its legality. Those who think that a grant for a term of years is annulled by the confirmed illness of the grantee are of opinion that the grant for life is void, while those again who think differently on that point, are of opinion that it is quite lawful. But even they admit that the *Khiraj* may be resumed by the sovereign at any time at the end of the current year.

If the grant is for the life of the grantee, and to his successors and heirs after his death, it is absolutely void; because by such an *Iktaa* the *Khiraj* would pass on from the rights of the public treasury to become an hereditary property.[4] The *Iktaa* being void *ab initio*, the

[1] P. 338. [2] *Ibid.* p. 339. [3] *Ib.* p. 340. [4] *Ibid.*

grantee must account for all he may have received by virtue of it. If the amount should exceed his allowance from the public treasury, he must restore the surplus, and if it be less he has a claim for the difference. The sovereign should intimate to the persons by whom the *Khiraj* is payable the invalidity of the *Iktaa*, and if after such notice they should continue to pay it to the grantee, they will still be liable for it to the public treasury.

Waste land. What has been said of *Iktaa* has reference only to the *Khiraj*. The land itself may be the subject of a grant in perpetuity, as in the case of *Ooshree* and *Wuzeefa* lands, which have become the property of private individuals. So also with regard to *Mookasumah* lands, the presumption being that they are still the property of the State, there seems to be no doubt that they may in like manner be granted to private persons and become their property, subject however to the *Khiraj* which may be assessed upon them. But, besides all these lands, there are, in many countries subject to Mussulman rule, large tracts of territory which have never been reclaimed from a state of nature, or if once reclaimed have fallen back again to their pristine condition, insomuch that it may be impossible to trace who ever were their proprietors. Such land is waste, and property in it is established by reclaiming it, **Property in, how acquired.** that is, by bringing it into cultivation, with the permission of the Imam, according to Aboo Huneefa, and by the mere act of reclaiming it, according to Aboo Yoosuf and Moohummud. When the two disciples concur in opinion against their master, the judge is in general at liberty to adopt whichever of the opinions he may think more conformable to sound reason and authority. But in India the preference has usually been given to the opinion of Aboo Huneefa. The Imam is accordingly said, in the *Futawa Alumgeeree,* to have the power of cutting off (*Iktaa*) waste land; but it is always to be kept in view, that, even according to Aboo Huneefa, it is not the Imam's permission that constitutes the proprietary right; for though a person should obtain such permission, and commence his operations by a partial clearance of the land, yet if he should discontinue them before the reclamation is completed, there would be no establishment of property, and any other person would be at liberty, after the expiration of three years, to enter upon the land and reclaim it, supposing that he obtains the permission of the Imam (p. 42). It is therefore the act of reclamation that constitutes the property, and as soon as that is completed the reclaimer becomes the lawful owner of the land, and may dispose of it at his pleasure; while, if undisposed of during his lifetime, it passes at his death, as a matter of course, to his heirs.

Waste land when reclaimed, liable to *Ooshr* or *Khiraj*.

Waste land when brought into cultivation by a Mooslim, is subject to *Ooshr* or *Khiraj*, according to its proximity to similar land, or its facilities of waters, as already explained; and it becomes immediately liable to one or other of these charges, though neither should be formally imposed upon it. The *Ooshr*, as well as the *Khiraj*, is appropriated by law to certain well-defined objects, from which there is no authority for saying that either can be lawfully diverted by the Imam, or his representative the sovereign of the country. The collections on account of both are to be brought into distinct departments of the *Beit-ool-mal* or public treasury. This, however, is not absolutely necessary; and the direct application of either cannot be considered a diversion from its legitimate objects. Accordingly it would seem that the *Ooshr* of a person's land may be lawfully given to the owner himself if he happens to be poor (p. 13); and we have seen that a similar application of the *Khiraj* is perfectly lawful when the owner of the land is one of the *Ahl* or people of *Khiraj*, provided that it does not extend beyond the life of the grantee. An hereditary grant of it being absolutely void, a perpetual exemption from it of any land that is legally subject to it must, by parity of reason, be equally so. Such exemption therefore of waste land, when brought into cultivation and otherwise liable to it, must be contrary to law; and there can thus be no such land as is

Cannot be exempted from *Khiraj* in perpetuity.

technically called *La-Khiraj*, that is, free from *Khiraj*, except land that is subject to *Ooshr*.

Application of *Khiraj* to India.

II. Having now said all that appeared to me to be necessary on the subject of the *Khiraj* generally, I proceed to enquire when and how it was applied to any part of the Provinces which now constitute the British Empire in India.

India was invaded on its north-west frontier by Mohammedans of the Hanifite sect at the beginning of the eleventh century of our era; but it was long before it can be said that the country was completely subdued.

In some places the native sovereigns submitted to pay tribute;[1] and the people being left under the government of their former rulers no change would necessarily take place in the ownership of the land. In much the greater part of the country, however, the native governments were at length entirely subverted, and the people were ultimately brought under the immediate rule of the conquerors. Wherever this took place the ownership of the land must be supposed to have passed, by the mere fact of conquest and operation of law, to the great body of the Mussulman community, represented in the particular place by the sovereign of the conquerors.

There is no record of the manner in which the land was disposed of at the time of the conquest of India. But it appears that in the time of Aurungzebe there was some land called *Ooshree* in the country (p. 74). That land, however, might have been originally waste, and brought into cultivation by Mussulmans under circumstances that would not render it liable to *Khiraj*; and at present the name of *Ooshree* land seems to be hardly known in India. On the whole, therefore, there does not seem to be any good reason for supposing that any considerable portion of the land was at the time of the conquest divided among

[1] Elphinstone, *Hist, of India*, p. 508,

First attempt to impose the *Khiraj* upon the land.

the soldiers of the conquering host. Nor does it appear with any degree of certainty that any attempt was made formally to impose the *Khiraj* upon any part of the land until the time of Ala-ood-deen, whose reign commenced about the year A.D. 1296. It is told of that sovereign by Ferishtah[1] that he ordered a tax equal to half the gross amount of the produce of the lands to be levied throughout the kingdom, and to be regularly transmitted to the Exchequer. The same fact is mentioned in the *Tareekh* of Feroze Shah,[2] where it is said of the same sovereign that he resolved there should be but one rule for the collection of tribute (*Khiraj*), and that all cultivation, whether on a small or large scale, was to be carried on by measurement at a certain rate for every *biswah*. Measurement is the basis of a *Wuzeefa*, and the operations of Ala-ood-deen look very like an attempt to impose the *Khiraj* in that form upon the land instead of the manner in which the revenue was previously raised. It does not appear very clearly how that was; but it is probable that it was levied partly by a division of the produce with the cultivator, and partly in the form of what was afterwards called a *Peshcush*, or something in the nature of a tribute from the chiefs or leading men of districts. The system of Ala-ood-deen was never completed, for it is said that his regulations came to an end after his death;[3] and it was not till after a long interval, or till the time of Shere Shah and Selim Shah, that any further attempt was made to impose a *Wuzeefa Khiraj* upon the land. These rulers are said in the *Ayeen Akbery* to be the first who actually abolished the custom of dividing crops[4] which must therefore have existed for some time, and probably before the operations of Ala-ood-deen, as already observed. The changes introduced by Shere Shah and Selim Shah were afterwards more fully developed in the system of Akbar, of which I now proceed to give a brief account.

System of Akbar.

The first step taken by him was to establish a uniform

[1] Briggs' *History*, vol. i. p. 346. [2] Elliott, vol. iii. p. 182.
[3] *Ibid.* p. 197. [4] Vol. i. p. 354.

standard of measure, to which the name of the *Ilahee Guz* was given, and it corresponded so nearly with the Arabian *zira* that it is considered in the Regulations of the Bengal Government as synonymous with it.[1] The land was then to be divided into square areas of 60 by 60 *guz*, which were called indifferently *jureeb* or *beegah*. So far the measures taken by Akbar were identical with those of Omar. The next step was to divide the lands into four kinds—*Poolej*, *Perowty*, *Checher*, and *Bunjer*. *Poolej* is land which is cultivated for every harvest, being never allowed to lie fallow. *Perowty* is land that is kept out of cultivation for a short time, in order that the land may recover its strength. *Checher* is land which, by reason of excessive rain or inundation, had lain fallow for four years. *Bunjer* is that which, for the same reason, had not been cultivated for five years. It was only to the first, or *Poolej* land, that a permanent tax like the *Wuzeefa* could be immediately applied. *Perowty* was not to be liable except when actually cultivated, but then it was to pay the same revenue as *Poolej*. For *Checher* land a progressive revenue was fixed, which began at two-fifths for the first year, and rose gradually to the fifth, when it became the same as *Poolej*; while for *Bunjer* land the revenue was to be four seers the *beegah* for the first year, and to rise progressively to the fifth year, when it also became fixed at the same rate as *Poolej*. *Poolej* being thus ultimately the standard for the four kinds of land, it was only farther necessary to ascertain the average produce of a *beegah* of such land, and then to determine the proportion of the produce that was to be taken for the revenue. The average was fixed by taking a third of the aggregate produce of good, bad, and middling *Poolej* land; and the revenue was then fixed at a third of that average.[2] Thus the aggregate produce of wheat on a *beegah* of good, bad and middling *Poolej*, being found to be 38 maunds and 35 seers, a third of that, or 12 maunds 38¼ seers, was the average; and a third of that again, or 4 maunds 12¾ seers, the revenue for a *beegah* of wheat. In like manner, the

[1] Wilson's *Glossary*, p. 567. [2] *Ay. Akb.* p. 355.

revenue for a *beegah* of rice was fixed at 4 maunds and 13 seers, and of cotton at 2 maunds and 20 seers; and so on for eleven different kinds of spring crops, and nineteen kinds of autumn crops; the revenue on each kind of produce being assessed at a fixed quantity of its own kind. The revenue being thus fixed in kind was made convertible into money at an average of the prices for nineteen years; and it was left optional to the husbandman to pay in money or in kind, that is, the fixed average third of each particular produce, or its fixed average price.[1]

But land being generally capable of yielding several kinds of crops, the revenue of any particular quantity, as a *beegah*, might be composed of different items, and vary from year to year with its actual produce. To avoid this a plan seems to have been very early adopted, if it was not coeval with the first assessment, of fixing the revenue at a lump sum for each *beegah*, determined, it is probable, according to an average of the crops for which it was supposed to be specially adopted. The revenue so fixed was called the *Toomar Jummah* and *Asul*, or original, as compared with subsequent additions to it.

Let us now compare the system of Akbar with what has been said of the *Wuzeefa Khiraj*. Of the four different kinds into which the land was divided, it was only *Perowty* that could not be brought under the conditions of that form of impost. It is true that it was not immediately applied to *Checher* and *Bunjer* also, but that was on account of the accidents of excessive rain and inundation to which they had been exposed, and sufficient allowance having been made on that account, they were thenceforth to be treated in the same way as *Poolej*, and would thus become permanently liable to *Khiraj*, which was the characteristic of the *Wuzeefa*. We need, therefore, have but little hesitation in saying that the impost levied by Akbar was the *Wuzeefa Khiraj* of the Mohammedan law, nor in deducing from it the same inference with regard to the property in the land that we have done in the case of that impost.

Akbar's impost really the *Wuzeefa Khiraj*.

[1] *Ay. Akb.* vol. i. p. 364.

But why, it may be asked, if the impost was in reality the *Wuzeefa*, was the name withheld, and no express reference made to the example of Omar. With regard to the name, it is to be observed that the chapter of the *Ayeen Akbery*, which contains a description of the system, is headed 'Of Tribute,' that is *Khiraj*, 'and Taxes,' which was probably thought sufficient; and a reason for omitting any reference to the example of Omar may be found in the fact that an assessment made in express conformity with his example could not be legally increased,[1] whereas the assessment of Akbar was limited to ten years. After the expiration of that term the rates might be increased, but that could not affect the right of property, which, we must conclude from the character of the *Wuzeefa Khiraj*, was transferred before the imposition of the tax to some persons who became liable for its payment. We must now endeavour to ascertain who these persons were.

Inference that persons liable for it became the proprietors of the land.

Who they were.

It has been already observed that the revenue, though convertible into money, might still be paid in kind at the option of the husbandman. This might be done in either of the methods known as *Kunkoot* and *Bhawely*, that is, by an estimate of the crops when standing, or by actual division of the grain when gathered into barns. This option being left to the husbandman points to him as the person immediately liable for the *Khiraj*. But further, the *Ayeen Akbery*, among other things, contains a description of the duties of certain great officers of the Empire, and among these the duties of the *Amil Guzzar* or collector of the revenue, for whose guidance very special instructions are given. In these he is directed to consider himself the immediate friend of the husbandman; 'to assist him with loans of money;' to transact his business with each husbandman separately, and 'see that the revenues are demanded with affability and complacency.' If any calamity befalls the crops the *Amil* shall immediately investigate the circumstances, make an exact calculation of the loss, and transmit the same to

[1] *Ante*, p. xxii.

the presence; and in particular he is instructed 'to agree with the husbandman to bring his rents himself at stated periods, that there may be no plea for employing intermediate mercenaries.' From all this it is sufficiently clear that the revenue, whatever it was, was payable by the ryots or cultivators direct to the State, and that they only were held to be liable for it. Hence we are in a manner constrained by the principles of the *Wuzeefa Khiraj* to infer that it was to these that the right of property in the land was transferred from the conquerors, and that consequently they became its proprietors.

Ryots or cultivators alone liable for the revenue under the system of Akbar.

Akbar's system not carried out as to whole of the land.

It was probably the intention of Akbar to have extended his system to the whole of the lands in his dominions. But that was never done; for in most of the *Soubahs* into which they were divided large tracts of land were left unmeasured. On these the public revenue was levied by a different rule technically understood under the Hindoo word *Buttai*, signifying division;[1] and, though the term *Mookasumah* may have been also applied to it by Mussulmans, as we know that there was some land called *Mookasumah* in the time of the Emperor Aurungzebe (pp. 74, 76) yet there is no evidence beyond the name that a *Mookasumah Khiraj* was ever formally imposed upon the land. Even though there were such evidence we should have no right, as already shown, to infer a preliminary grant of the land in that case, and must therefore conclude, with regard to the unmeasured lands, for want of evidence to the contrary, that they would still remain the property of the conquerors, or the sovereign as their representative.

Firman of Aurungzebe.

I have no means of tracing the tenure of land through the reigns of Jehangire and Shahjehan, but we have an important document of the time of Aurungzebe (p. 74), the son and successor of Shahjehan, from which it appears that the tenure and position of the ryots, or cultivators, was pretty much the same at that time as it had been left by Akbar. This document is a firman which was intended

[1] Ap. F. R. p. 638.

for the guidance of the officers employed in the collection of the revenue 'throughout the protected dominions of Hindoostan, from one extremity to the other.' It follows very closely the instructions of Akbar to his *Amil Guzzars* for the treatment of the ryots, or husbandmen. But in the firman we have the distinction strongly marked between the two kinds of *Khiraj*, leaving no doubt that the rate imposed by Akbar was a true *Wuzeefa*. In the firman it is called *Mowezzef*, but this is only a different inflexion from the same root, having the same meaning. From the frequency with which this term occurs in the firman, as compared with *Mookasumah*, it would seem that a great deal more of the land had been measured and brought under the system of Akbar than had been accomplished by Akbar himself. Moreover, what was only an inference from the imposition of the *Wuzeefa* in the case of Akbar's settlement, has now become a reality; for at every step the ryots or husbandmen are treated as the proprietors of the land where the *Khiraj* is *Mowezzef*. Thus, first, to show that the rate was levied in the same way as that of Akbar, on different kinds of crops, we have the following direction in the eighth paragraph: 'The season for demanding the *Khiraj Mowezzef* on every species is when the harvest is fit for reaping; therefore, for every particular species that shall come at that state they shall take the proportion of tribute.' Again, to show that it, and consequently the rate of Akbar, was a true *Wuzeefa*, we have in the tenth paragraph the following: 'Whosoever, notwithstanding he possesses the ability to cultivate his own land, and meets with no impediment, nevertheless suffers it to be uncultivated, let them exact the tribute from other means;' which is the very characteristic of that form of the *Khiraj*. Further, to show that the ryots or husbandmen are treated as the proprietors of the land, we have, in the second paragraph: 'They (the officers) shall acquire information of the proprietors of the land from whom this tribute is to be collected, whether they cultivate or not.' In the next paragraph, we have: 'In *Khiraj Mowezzef*, if the proprietor of the land, for want of means of pro-

Treats the ryots as proprietors of *Wuzeefa* land.

viding the implements of husbandry, has been unable to cultivate.' Not to multiply extracts, I will only further quote the following from the sixth paragraph: 'In a case of *Khiraj Mowezzef*, they shall settle for such a rate that the ryots may not be ruined by the lands; and they shall not on any account exact beyond (the value of) half of the produce, notwithstanding any (particular) ability to pay more.' This extract is further of importance because it defines very clearly what was the ryot's tenure. When the *Khiraj* was *Mowezzef* he was proprietor of the land, but subject to a variable rate up to the value of one half of the produce, that is, after the expiration of the ten years' settlement by Akbar.

I have said in an early part of this essay that it is only where the *Khiraj* is *Wuzeefa* that we have any right to infer the existence of a right of property previous to its imposition in the party by whom it is payable. There may possibly, however, be some such right where the *Khiraj* is *Mookasumah*, though we are not entitled to infer it. And we know that, with the consent of the sovereign and the ryot, a change may be made from *Wuzeefa* to *Mookasumah* (pp. 7 and 75). So that what appears to be *Mookasumah* land might have been originally *Wuzeefa*, and may therefore still be the property of the person in possession of it. Not only so, but a change may, with the like consent, be made from *Mookasumah* to *Wuzeefa*. So that it would seem that the holder of *Mookasumah* land may have some sort of permanent interest in the land, though it may fall short of the full right of property enjoyed by the holder of *Wuzeefa*. Thus we find the holder of *Mookasumah* land *treated* as a *quasi* proprietor in the firman of Aurungzebe, where we have, towards the end, the following words. 'In *Khiraj Mokossimeh*, every one who is not the (hereditary) proprietor of such *Khiraj* land, whether infidel or Mussulman, having bought it or taken it in mortgage, shall receive the profits with permission (of Government).' I have said *quasi* proprietor, because it seems from this that, though the possessor of *Mookasumah* land was entitled to enjoy it himself, and transmit it to his heirs, he could neither sell nor mortgage it without the permission of the Government. No such permission could of course be legally requisite in the case of a sale or mortgage by the holder of *Wuzeefa* land. Nor do we find that any attempt to enforce such restriction upon him had been made in the time of Aurungzebe; for, in the thirteenth paragraph of the firman, we have these words: 'In *Khiraj Mowezzef*, if a person sells a part of his own such tributary land, and the buyer has taken possession (seeing that), if he wishes to cultivate in that year, nobody can hinder him, &c.' And again, towards the end of the next paragraph, we have these words: 'If an infidel sells his land to a Mussulman, they shall exact from him *Khiraj Mowezzef*.' In these cases no allusion is made to the permission of Government. So that it would appear that down to the time of Aurungzebe, no attempt had been made to reduce the condition of the holder of *Wuzeefa* land from his full proprietary rights, though that of the *Mookasumah* holder seems to have been so much raised as to leave little distinction between him and the *Wuzeefa* holder, except that while the latter could dispose of his land by sale or mortgage at pleasure, the former could do so only with the permission of the Government. This will prepare us for the disappearance of that distinction, and the substitution of another, as we come down to later times.

The assessment of Akbar was limited to the value of a third of the produce of the land, and it would seem, *primâ facie*, that the ryot must have been free to retain the whole of the remaining two-thirds for his own benefit. But that did not follow as a matter of course. There might have been some other party entitled, by custom or virtue of some right recognised by the ryot, to a portion of it; and the difference between a third and a half of the produce, which the law considered generally sufficient for the maintenance of the cultivator and his family, or one sixth of the whole, might thus have been left for the benefit of such other party, though in strictness he could have no legal right to it after the ryot had become the proprietor of the land.

Zemindars. In the *Ayeen Akbery*, mention is made of a class of persons called Zemindars, as forming an important part of the Military Force of the Empire. In Bengal they are described as furnishing large bodies of cavalry and infantry, besides cannon, boats, and elephants; while the Soubah of Berar is said to be full of them, and they are described as being very powerful in Ajmeer. Speaking generally of the Army of the Empire, the Zemindary troops alone are said to have been upwards of four millions. The word Zemindar, or more correctly *Zumeen-dar*, is a compound of two Persian words, *Zumeen* (land) and *dar* (holder), and means literally a holder of land. The name, therefore, could hardly have been given to any class of persons who had no recognised connection with the land; while the above descriptions of them preclude the idea of their being the ryots or cultivators. Further, it is difficult to imagine how in those ages such large bodies of troops could be maintained unless their supplies had been derived in some way from the land; which would imply some degree of power over it or its occupants in the persons who were obliged to furnish them.

In the *Mulfoozat Timooree*, or Memoirs of Timour, we meet with frequent notices of powerful chiefs, sometimes submitting to that Emperor on his invasion of India, and as often in rebellion against him. In a Persian translation of that work made in the reign of Shah Jehan, these chiefs are called *Zemindars*; and if we may assume that the persons so styled belong to the same class as the persons to whom the name is applied in the *Ayeen Akbery*, the account which is given of one of them in particular in the *Mulfoozat*, may perhaps afford some insight into the secret of that power which enabled them to support so large a number of retainers. The individual alluded to was a Zemindar called Malik Shaikha of the family of Kokhlar. His brother Nasrut had been formerly Governor

[1] *Ay. Akb.* vol. i. p. 239.

of Lahor on the part of Sultan Mahmoud of Delhi, and after his defeat Malik Shaikha 'had been the first of all the Zemindars and Governors of Hindoostan,' to give in his submission to the conqueror. For this reason Timour observes of him in the Memoirs, 'I was very considerate for his subjects, and whenever any *Zemindar* of that country represented himself to be a dependent of Shaikha Kokhlar, I protected him from the assaults of my followers, and from pillage and plunder.'[1] Shaikha, it seems, remained in attendance on the Emperor from 'his capture of Delhi till his passage of the Jumna;' but then, having asked for and obtained permission to return to Lahor, 'he forgot his protestations of service and devotion,' and princes and Amirs were sent to 'take that ungrateful man prisoner, and to levy a ransom from Lahor.' In reply to their report, the Emperor proceeds: 'I wrote that as Shaikha had proved false to his engagements, his country was to be plundered and himself sent in chains to my presence.' From this account it appears that there were at that time two kinds of Zemindars—one superior, having a country and subjects, and the other inferior or dependent; and it is at least probable that the former may have been the successors of ancient Rajahs, or rulers of the country; while the latter were subordinate chiefs, or perhaps proprietors, of the country; and that both the superior and inferior had been left at the first conquest of the country in the possession of some of the powers which they originally had in their particular districts, so far as was consistent with a general subjection to the conquerors. **Superior and inferior Zemindars.**

This conjecture derives some confirmation from the fact that, at the time of the perpetual settlement of the revenue in Bengal, Behar and Orissa, there were still superior and inferior Zemindars,[2] the latter of whom were more or less dependent on the former, and that some of the great Zemindaries even now descend, as being in the nature of sovereignties, by primogeniture, instead of being divisible according to Hindoo and Mohammedan law.

[1] Elliott, vol. iii. p. 473.

[2] Ap. F. R. p. 456.

Moreover, the conjecture accounts in some degree for the duties which have always been understood to be incumbent on the Zemindars, of keeping up the roads and protecting travellers in their districts, and also for their responsibilities on account of thefts and robberies committed within them.

Supposing the superior Zemindars to represent the original Rajahs or sovereigns of the country, they would under the Hindoo law have been entitled to a share in the produce of the land. But, 'this being limited to a sixth, or at most a fourth, there must (as observed by Mr. Elphinstone) have been another proprietor for the remaining five-sixths or three-fourths, who must obviously have had the greatest interest of the two.' The ryots or cultivators would, no doubt, have had some, perhaps the greatest, part of these shares; yet if they had the whole, it would seem that they would in the course of time have risen above the condition of mere tillers of the ground, so as ultimately to have others of that class under them. It does not appear, however, that any such change has taken place in their condition, which seems to have been pretty much the same in all ages. For this reason it appears to me probable that there were others to participate with them in the shares of the produce left untouched by their kings, and that those parties were the class of persons afterwards known as inferior Zemindars, or Chowdhries, who would otherwise have been unprovided for. All rights or interests in the land or its produce were extinguished by the Mussulman conquest, but the conquerors for a considerable time after their first invasion appear to have cared for little but revenue. The easiest and simplest way for obtaining that was to leave the civil government of the country with the native chiefs, supreme or inferior, in whose hands they found it, and to employ them in the collection of the revenues already established in the country. Accordingly, we find from *Ferishtah* that so late as the reign of the Sultan Mahomed Shah, in the year 1438, use was made in some such manner of the Zemindars, whom we have supposed to be the successors or representatives of these chiefs; for the historian, speaking of the distracted state of affairs, says: 'The farmers and Zemindars, foreseeing the convulsions that were likely to ensue, withheld their revenues, in the hopes of retaining them.'[1] I suppose things to have remained in this state for a considerable time; the conquerors being satisfied with what could thus be obtained through the Zemindars until they found their government sufficiently established to enable them to impose their own system of revenue, that is the *Khiraj*, upon the land. Whenever that took place it would have created a revolution in the condition of the Zemindars. Indeed, to depress, if not entirely to extinguish them, seems to have been one of the principal motives which led Ala-ood-deen to impose, as already mentioned, a tax equal to half the annual produce of the lands throughout the kingdom. At that time it would seem that estimates of the produce were required from the Zemindars, and that superintendents were appointed over the collectors, 'to take care that the Zemindars should demand no more from the cultivators than the estimates the Zemindars themselves had made.'[2] And so effectual were these and the other oppressive measures of Ala-ood-deen, that many were left without any money, till at length it came to pass 'that, excepting *Maliks* and *Amirs*, officials and *Multanis*, no one possessed even a trifle in cash.'[3]

The Zemindars are not mentioned among the exceptions, and it may be presumed that they were reduced to the same dead level of poverty as the rest of the community. The various regulations of Ala-ood-deen came to naught at his death, as already observed, and the extreme pressure on the cultivators being thus removed, a margin of produce would again be left to the Zemindar, who might then rise to the condition in which he was afterwards found at the invasion of Timour. It is further probable that he remained in that state, not only to the time of Mahomed

[1] Briggs's *Ferishtah*, vol. i. p. 537. [2] *Ibid.* p. 346.
[3] Elliott, vol. iii. p. 179.

Shah, but also down to that of Selim Shah and Akbar, which will account for his palmy condition at the latter period, when he was able to contribute so largely to the military force of the empire.

Condition of Zemindars varied with the demands of the state on the produce of the land.

In this view the condition of the ryot may be supposed generally to remain pretty much the same under all circumstances, while that of the Zemindar would sink with every fresh demand on the produce of the land. About the commencement of the reign of Aurungzebe, that is, in the year A.D. 1658, an addition was made to the *Asul Toomar jummah* in Bengal during the administration of Shah Shujah. But so great was the Emperor's 'economy, which allowed no expense for the luxury and ostentation of a Court,' and such 'the skill and vigilance with which he managed the disbursements of the State,' that they 'afforded him a resource for the wants of his people, without pressing heavily on their means.'[1] Accordingly, we do not hear of any addition to the revenues during the remainder of his reign. Amid the anarchy that followed soon after his death, a number of *de facto* governments were established throughout the country, and the pressure on the land may thus be supposed to have varied with the exigencies and characters of the rulers in particular localities. At some places in the North-Western Provinces the pressure became so great, that scarcely any of the produce seems to have been left with the cultivators, beyond what was necessary for the subsistence of themselves and their families, and the Zemindars were reduced to a condition very little above that of the ordinary ryots. There is no reason to suppose that the demand on the land was less in Bengal than elsewhere. But during the administration of Jaffier Khan, or from A.D. 1711 to A.D. 1726, a great revolution took place in the state of the Zemindars, for there was 'a universal dispossession of the Zemindars,'[2] and a re-arrangement was made of the Provinces into official Zemindaries, in which some of the original Zemindaries seem to have been included, though under the

[1] Mill's *Hist.* vol. ii. p. 395. [2] Ap. F. R. p. 189.

name of Talooks or dependencies. These official Zemin-daries were constituted by *Sunnuds*, from the terms of which it appears that the Zemindars were no longer charged with any military duties, but had become *Amils* or collectors of the public revenue ; for in the details of their duties, it is expressly stated that they are to 'deliver into the treasury at proper times the due rent of the Sircar,' and that after the expiration of the year 'they take a discharge according to custom, and that they deliver the account of their Zemindary, agreeable to the stated forms, every year, into the Duftar Cana of the Sircar.' Deductions were allowed for certain known charges called *muzkoorat*, which varied in different Zemindaries, but always included what was called a *nankar* or bread allowance for the Zemindar himself, and very generally similar provisions called *neemtucky* and *mocudemy* for the *Kanoongoes* and head men of the villages. The *nankar* was commonly estimated at about ten per cent. of the collections.[1] The *Sunnud* usually contained a consideration called *peshcush*, for which it was said to be granted. In the *Sunnud* to the East India Company for the Zemindary of the 24 Pergunnahs the *peshcush* was Rs. 20,101, while in that to Chitun Sing for the Pergunnah of Bishenpoor, the *peshcush* to the British Government, by whom the *Sunnud* was granted, was 186 mohurs and two anas. The Zemindary having become an office, was naturally limited to the life of the person to whom the *Sunnud* was granted, but was frequently renewed to the son of the Zemindar by a fresh *Sunnud*, which, however, was not issued until the payment of the *peshcush*. In Behar there was a re-adjustment of the *Asul Toomar jummah*, as well as in Bengal, but it did not take place till 1685 ; and some re-arrangement of the province into official Zemindaries seems also to have been subsequently made, though not to the same extent as in Bengal. According to Mr. Shore there were only three great Zemindaries in which the

[1] Mr. Shore's Min. Ap. F. R. p. 184.

Zemindar could be considered the *Amil* or collector on behalf of the government.[1] In all the others the revenue was collected direct from the ryots by *Amils* appointed by the government;[2] though the *Amils* are said to have availed themselves[3] of the assistance of persons called *Maliks*, who seem to have been the same as those known in Bengal under the name of talookdars.[4] The condition of the *Maliks* was so much reduced that they are described as being glad to receive what was called *malikanah* or proprietary right, that is ten per cent., whether on the collections or on the whole produce does not distinctly appear. The word *malik* means literally proprietor (though the name had been given in earlier times to great officers of the state), and indicates that the persons to whom the term was applied were still held in popular estimation to be in some sense proprietors, though any proprietorship that their ancestors may have originally possessed in the land was extinguished at the Mohammedan conquest, and the land had not been re-granted to them, but to the persons on whom the responsibility for the *Khiraj* was imposed, that is the ryots or cultivators, as has been already observed.

Ryots.

The condition of the ryots seems to have remained meanwhile pretty much the same as it had always been. The word *Mookasumah* was lost in the Hindoo word *Buttae*, and as that form of the *Khiraj* does not seem to have prevailed to any extent in Bengal, the ryots came to be distinguished only according as the lands which they cultivated did or did not belong to the village in which they reside. The former were called *Khood-kasht* the latter *Pae-kasht*; words which are still in common use, though more properly applicable to the land than to the cultivators. *Khood-kasht* is a compound of two Persian words, *Khood*, self—and *Kasht*, a contraction of *Kashtu* sown—and means literally self-sown, which is somewhat ambiguous. But the true meaning of the expression is well brought out in the following translation by Mr.

[1] Ap. F. R. p. 452. [2] *Ibid.* p. 451. [3] *Ibid.* [4] *Ib.* p. 452.

Gladwin of an edict by Jehangire:[1]—'The officers of the *Khalsa* and Jageerdars are positively prohibited from the practice of forcibly taking the ryots' lands and *cultivating them for their own benefit*: the words which I have put into italics being in the original *Khoodkasht sazund* or 'make them *Khoodkasht*.' So that a *Khoodkasht* ryot must be one who sows for his own benefit. *Paekasht*, according to the author of the *Indian Glossary*, means sown by a *pae*, which again is only a non-resident cultivator; but as the word is opposed to *Khoodkasht* it would seem to indicate, when applied to a ryot, one who does not cultivate for himself but for another, as, for example, on hire. According to Mr. Shore, the *Khoodkasht* ryots, either from length of occupancy or other cause, have a stronger right than others, and may in some sense be considered as hereditary tenants;'[2] while 'the other class or *Paekasht*' are considered as tenants at will, and have only a temporary accidental interest in the soil which they cultivate.'[3] Mr. Shore says, at the same time, that there was a class of ryots who were 'compelled to stand to all losses, and to pay for the land whether cultivated or not, and, as the *Paekasht* could not be that class, and only two classes are mentioned, it follows that it must have been the *Khoodkasht* who were compelled to pay for the land whether cultivated or not. But that was the very characteristic of the holder of the *Wuzeefa* land, and the *Khoodkasht* ryot can be none other than his successor or representative, and must, consequently, on the principles of the Mohammedan law, be the actual proprietor of the land, and not merely a hereditary tenant, if there could be any such thing under that law, understanding by tenant one who holds the property of another.[4] All, however, that is necessarily implied in that proprietorship is a right to the productive powers of the soil, without which he would not be able to meet his liability for the *Khiraj*. It would be straining the law too far to

[1] *Hist.* p. 98. [2] Ap. F. R. p. 192. [3] *Ibid.*
[4] See *Hedaya*, vol. iii. p. 367.

suppose that the ryot necessarily became entitled to the minerals contained in the soil.

Jaghires—early history.

Having now brought down the Zemindar and the ryots to the close of the Mohammedan period, it only remains to inquire how the *Khiraj*, or the Government's share in the produce of the land, was disposed of with reference to its effect on the tenure of the land.

In early times a practice seems to have arisen of paying officials, chiefly military, by temporary grants of land, or the revenue derived from it. Thus, so far back as the reign of Shums-ood-deen, or say between A.D. 1211 and A.D. 1236, mention is made of two thousand horsemen who had received grants of villages in the Doab by way of pay. About thirty or forty years later, many of these grants were resumed by Sultan Gheias-ood-deen Bulbul;[1] but the practice seems to have continued more or less till the time of Ala-ood-deen, who is said to have entirely disapproved of it, and paid his followers every year with money from the treasury.[2] The practice nevertheless was revived under Sultan Feroze, who succeeded to the throne of Delhi A.D. 1351, and is said to have shown great liberality in his grants of revenue, instead of salaries or pecuniary allowances: 'to some giving 10,000 tunkas, to others 5,000, and to others 2,000, according to the respective ranks and claims of the different office-bearers. These grants were called *Nanha*, a word which literally signifies breads, being the plural of the Persian word *nan*.

This was anterior to the invasion of Timour; but we find in the *Institutes* of that monarch mention of similar grants under the name of *Yetool*. In the translation of that work into Persian, which was made in the time of Jehangir, the son and successor of Akbar, the word is rendered by the term *Jageer*, and the holder of the *Yetool* is termed the *Jageerdar*. These names had already been in use in the time of Akbar, for they occur in the *Ayeen Akbery*, and the practice of making grants of that

[1] Elliott, vol. iii. pp. 107–8.

[2] *Ibid.* p. 289.

description had been carried to such an extent that under the denomination of *Jageer* 'near two-fifths of the territory' are said to have been 'assigned under temporary tenures for the support of the provincial civil and military establishments.'[1]

Division of the country under Akbar into *Khalsa* and *Jaghire.*

The whole kingdom after the assessment of Akbar is thus described by Mr. James Grant, in his able survey of the Northern Circars,[2] as being distributed into two great divisions. The first of these comprised the 'lands that were immediately dependent on the *Khalsa Shereefa*, or royal exchequer,' and which were 'set apart to defray the personal and court expenses of the Emperor, those of his guards and state garrisons, as well as the similar establishments of all his delegated representatives throughout the Empire.' The other division comprehended such lands 'as were assigned over to the greater or lesser officers of the Government, for the maintenance of troops and personal dignities by a feudal tenure first called *Atka*,[3] then Jageer, signifying territorial possessions so alienated at the will and during the precarious favour of a despotic monarch.' These lands, 'though generally distinguished by the Arabic term *Atka*, or the synonymous Persian word Jageer, yet received various more particular denominations from the nature of the different tenures on which they were held.' Thus, the assignments to the greater officers of Government were called Foujdarees. By *foujdary* was understood 'a simple allotment of an extensive territory, with its jurisdiction and revenue, to a *foujdar*, or military commander, for a limited or indefinite period, under an express obligation of maintaining a certain body of troops to attend the king in person, or any of his lieutenants, in the field.' So also the assignments to the lesser officers of government, which were 'commonly confined to a single Circar,' were called *Tycul.* This word, according to the author of the *Indian Glossary* is 'no doubt a typographical error for *Tayool*' (a word which has come down to our

[1] Ap. F. R. p. 253. [2] *Ibid.* p. 639.

[3] Properly *Akta*, or *Ikta*; see *ante*, p. xxiv.

times in connection with the villages conferred on the Kings of Delhi by the East India Company, as a sort of appanage for the support of themselves and dependents); and this seems to me to be highly probable. But I cannot agree with the learned author in assuming that the latter word is a derivative from an Arabic root which means 'support'; for though that occurs as one of the meanings of the root, it is not its ordinary meaning, and the derivative has quite a different signification both in Arabic and Persian. Moreover, the word does not occur in the *Ayeen Akbery*, nor does it appear to be naturalised in the Hindoostanee language.[1] I am, therefore, inclined to think that it is rather a misprint or misreading of the Tartar word *yetool*, which we have already met with as a synonym for Jageer. The Foujdarees were military governments for the purpose of guarding the frontier provinces of the empire, and had been abolished, or mixed up with the greater Zemindaries at the time of the transfer of the general government of Bengal to the East India Company. They may therefore be left out of consideration, together with the *Khalsa Shereefa*, as having no bearing on the tenure of land, and our attention is thus confined to what may be called the *Jaghire* proper; that is the assignments to the lesser officers, originally termed *Yetool*, though subsequently known under the former name.

Meaning of Jaghire.

The word Jaghire, or more correctly *Jageer*, is a compound of two Persian words, *ja* (place) and *geer* (contraction of *geerindah*, taker), the compound being thus properly a participle, signifying 'place taker,' though it is commonly used as a substantitive noun, the word *dar*, or holder, being added, to signify the person who holds the jageer, as jageerdar. The word necessarily implies a holding in some sense of a particular place; for, as the object of the grant was the maintenance of a certain number of troops, it was necessary that the person who undertook to maintain them should have such a command over the place from which the revenue for their mainte-

[1] It is not found in the dictionaries.

nance was to be derived, as to enable him to enforce the payment of the revenue by the persons who were liable for it. The Jageerdar was thus, in a manner, 'substituted exactly in the place of the government,' and acquired 'immediately and during the legal continuance of his grant all the jurisdictions, rights and prerogatives belonging to the sovereign.'[1] But this was only 'when a whole district was made over to him,' so as to entitle him 'to the full yearly crown-rent.' When, on the other hand, only 'a stated amount of money is assigned (in *daums* or rupees) issuing partially from territorial resources of revenue, then the Jageerdar is restricted entirely to the emoluments of his pecuniary income, and can have no local influence whatever, in consequence, 'within the limits of his grant.'[2] He had thus no direct means of vindicating his right to the allowance granted to him, and his grant accordingly contained a requisition to the officials and ryots of the district on which it was assigned to account to him for the rents and dues to the full amount of the assignment. The Jaghires referred to in Regulation XIII. of 1830, and Act XIII. of 1842 of the Bombay Code, seem to have been of the first description. So also the Jageer of the late Begum Sumroo in Sirdhanah. And in No. IV. of the Appendix we have a Perwanneh addressed to the agent of a Jageerdar apparently of the same kind, requiring him to do justice to a complaint, as if there was no doubt of his having the power to do so. Jageers of this description being burdened with services to be rendered, were called *mushroot* or *shurtee* (conditional); while those of the other kind, being entirely gratuitous, or in recompense for services already performed, were termed *bila shurt*, or without condition. Accordingly, Lord Clive's Jaghire of 222,958 rupees on the 24 Pergunnahs, which was of that description, was expressly said to be unconditional; and it contained a requisition to the East India Company, as Zemindars of the district, 'to pay their rents to Lord

[1] Ap. F. R. p. 408. [2] *Ibid.*

Clive as Jaghirdar, in like manner as they were before bound to do to the established Government.' Nos. II. and III. of the Appendix may also be cited as examples of unconditional jageers, and they both contain requisitions of the like kind to the officials and ryots of the districts to account for the rents up to the full amounts granted to the *quasi* jageerdars.

Seyurghal. Under the head of assigned lands were also included alienations known by the name of *Seyurghal*,[1] which had increased to a very considerable extent previously to the time of Akbar. The word is of Tartar origin, and the persons in whose favour grants under that name were made are described in the *Ayeen Akbery* as being divided into four classes: 1st, the learned and their scholars; 2nd, those who had bid adieu to the world; 3rd, the needy who are not able to help themselves; 4th, the descendants of great families, who, from a sense of false shame, will not submit to follow any occupation for their support. The allowances to these persons were sometimes in the form of *Tunkhas*, or assignments on the revenue of particular localities, and sometimes in the form of grants of land, which were called *milk* and *mudd-al-mash*;[2] terms, the former of which signifies *property*, and the latter 'prolonging of life.' The *Tunkhas* were essentially unconditional Jageers, and therefore necessarily limited to the lives of the grantees. The same may be said of the *revenue* derivable from the lands; and though grants of lands are hereditary in their own nature, yet being gifts they are revokable by Mohammedan law at any timeduring the life of the grantee, and might thus be considered temporary, in the same way as the revenues derived from them. Wherever the grant was not revoked, it would pass at the death of the grantee to his heirs. And thus we find, in the *Ayeen Akbery*, reference to some grants of *Seyurghal* that were treated as hereditary. For the better regulation of *Seyurghal* grants, a rule was estab-

[1] Erroneously written *Sycurghal* in Ap. F. R. p. 639.

[2] *Ay. Akb.* vol. i. p. 128.

lished[1] that where the grant was of land the land was to be half arable, and the other half capable of being brought into cultivation; a rule, of which two examples will be found in Nos. V. and VI. of the Appendix. Where, again, the grant was in the form of an assignment over land, the whole of which was arable, a fourth part of the revenue was to be deducted, and a *Tunkha* issued for only three-fourths.[2]

Melkeyut.

Besides the *Jageer* and *Seyurghal*, there is mention in the *Ayeen Akbery* of another grant called *Melkeyut.* It occurs in the enumeration of certain purposes for which the *Firman Subtee* was used. Eight great offices are mentioned for appointments to which that *Firman* was issued, and then we have these words: 'also for the grant of a *jageer Sir* or *tun*; for confirming the salaries of officers in conquered territories; for granting a *Melkeyut;* for a grant *Seyurghal.*' The *Firman Subtee* required the seal of the sovereign, as well as the signatures of his ministers. There were two seals in use in Akbar's time, one small and the other large. 'The small one, which is called *ouzek*, is used for stamping of firmans, and the larger one, on which are also engraven the names of His Majesty's predecessors, is used for letters to foreign princes.'[3] It must have been the *ouzek*, then, that was attached to all grants of *jageer*, *melkeyut*, and *seyurghal.* The only other mention of *melkeyut* that I have met with is in the following extract from Mr. Gladwin's history of Jehangir, (p. 100): 'The Emperors his predecessors (he says), whenever they bestowed a *jageer* in *melkyet* or *perpetuity*, were used to affix to the patent a red seal, from whence such a grant was called *Altumgha.* Jehangier directed that, instead of red ink, the impression should be taken in gold leaf, whence it was afterwards called Altoon Tumgha.' From the above account of Akbar's seals, there can be little doubt that the *Altumgha* was only the *ouzek* used with red ink; as, indeed, Mr. Gladwin himself says in another place (p. 13), 'the *ouzek* is affixed to all

Altumgha.

[1] *Ay. Akb.* vol. i. pp. 283-4. [2] *Ibid.* [3] *Ibid.* p. 67.

firmans.' If Mr. Gladwin's account of the *Altumgha* be correct, then it would seem that a Jageer, which was only a temporary grant of revenue, and could not be lawfully extended beyond the life of the grantee, might, by a mere change of the colour of a seal, be converted into an estate of inheritance. But Mr. Gladwin's rendering of the word *melkeyet* (or more properly *milkiyut*) by 'perpetuity' is not correct; for the only meanings given of the word in Johnson's *Arabic and Persian Dictionary*, and in Shakespear's *Hindustanee Dictionary*, are 'property, possession, use, right.' And if the expression *jageer* in *melkeyet* is to be found in any native writer, it can only be understood as meaning a grant in property, that is, a grant of the property or land from which the jageer or right to revenue is derived. In this sense the grant of a jageer might, perhaps, with some looseness of expression, be said to be in perpetuity, and this is probably all that Mr. Gladwin really meant; for the owner of the land would be left to appropriate the revenue to himself, and the same liberty be continued to his heirs, so long as they were not called upon to account for it by the successors of the grantor. That this is all that could be assured to the grantee, or, indeed, was ever pretended to be bestowed by grants in *Altumgha*, is, I think, made clear by the two following examples of *Altumgha* grants by the Emperor, Shah Alum, to the East India Company. The first is of the Dewanny of the Province of Bengal, dated 12th August 1765, which after stating, 'We have granted them, as a free gift and Ultumgau, the office of the Dewanny of the *Khalsa Shereefa* of the Province of Bengal,' proceeds as follows: 'It is requisite that our royal descendants, the viziers, the bestowers of dignity, the Omrahs high in rank,' &c., 'as well the future as the present, using their constant endeavours for the establishment of this our Royal command, leave the said office in possession of the said Company from generation to generation, for ever and ever.' The other is a firman confirming the grants of Burdwan and the rest of the Company's possessions in Bengal, bearing the same date of the 12th August, 1765.

Two examples of *Altumgha*.

After reciting the original grants to the said Company in the time of Meer Mahomed Kassim and Meer Mahomed Jaffier Khan deceased, it proceeds: 'We, in consideration of the attachment of the said Company, have been graciously pleased to confirm to them, as a free gift and ultumgau, without the association of any other.' Then follows the request to 'our royal descendants,' &c., exactly in the same terms as the last firman. Now, if the *Altumgha* grant conferred in itself a hereditary right, there would have been no occasion for these special clauses. But as Shah Alum had no power to bind his successors to a perpetual alienation of the *Khiraj* or land revenue, which was contrary to the Mohammedan law, an appeal to their forbearance became necessary to give even the semblance of perpetuity to his grants, so far as the revenue was concerned, though, with regard to the land, the right of resumption might, as already mentioned, be barred by the death of the original grantees.

Tenures of land under the British Government.

III. Having brought the different interests in the land or its produce down to the acquisition of the Lower Provinces by the East India Company, we have now to enquire how far these interests were affected by the perpetual settlement of the revenue in those Provinces, which took place in 1793 under the administration of Lord Cornwallis.

The Government having determined to commute its share in the produce of the land into payments of money to be fixed in perpetuity, it was thought desirable that the settlement should be made with the proprietors of the land, whoever they might happen to be. I have offered some reasons for inferring that the *Khoodkasht* ryots, as representing the original holders of *Wuzeefa* land, had the best title to be considered the owners of so much of the land as may have been brought under the system of Akbar. But their proprietary rights were entirely ignored by the two rival authorities of the period—Mr. Shore, afterwards Lord Teignmouth, and Mr. James Grant. By the former the Zemindars and certain Talookdars who paid their revenue direct to the Government, were deemed to be the proprietors;[1] while Mr. Grant considered the Government itself to be the proprietor, and the Zemindars only its officers. Yet, at the same time, it seems to have been generally allowed that the *Khoodkasht* ryots had some sort of hereditary 'privilege of holding possession of the spots of land which they cultivate so long as they pay the revenue assessed upon them.'[2] But Mr. Shore supposed this privilege, or right of occupancy as he termed it, to have been acquired by long possession under pottahs granted by the Zemindars.[3] The difference between the *Khoodkasht* ryots and the *paekasht* ryots he supposed to have arisen from a difference in their pottahs; those to the latter containing a limitation of time,[4] while the pottahs to the former were indefinite in that respect.

Perpetual settlement of revenue in the Lower Provinces with Zemindars and Talookdars as proprietors of the soil.

The views of Mr. Shore seem to have influenced the measures of Lord Cornwallis, and a settlement of the revenue for ten years was made with the Zemindars and certain Talookdars, as the actual proprietors of the soil. The settlement was afterwards made perpetual, though contrary to the opinion of Mr. Shore, and the rules under which it had been concluded were re-enacted in Regulation VIII. of 1793. *Chowdries* are also mentioned in that Regulation as a denomination of proprietors, but the name does not occur again in the Regulation, and as it has now dropped out of use, they may be left out of consideration. If there were any Talookdars at that time whose revenue was paid direct to the Government, as stated by Mr. Shore, they were not distinguished from the Zemindars, from whom, indeed, they would differ only in name. But there were other Talookdars whose revenue was paid through the Zemindars. Of these there were two classes, called Independent and Dependent. The Independent were those 'who had purchased their lands or obtained them by gift, and had received deeds of sale or gift of such lands, or sunnuds from the Khalsa, making over the proprietary rights to them.' These were allowed

Independent and dependent, or *Pottah*, Talookdars.

[1] Ap. F. R. p. 205.

[2] Minute by Lord Cornwallis, Ap. F. R. p. 487.

[3] *Ibid.* p. 206. [4] *Ibid.* p. 207.

to settle for their lands directly with the Government. The Dependant Zemindars, on the other hand, were supposed to hold their Talooks under writings or sunnuds which did not expressly transfer the property in the soil, but only entitled 'the Talookdar to possession so long as he continued to discharge the rent or perform the conditions stipulated therein,' and they 'were considered as leaseholders only, not actual proprietors of the soil.' They, therefore, were not to be separated from the Zemindar, or other actual proprietor from whom they derived their tenures, and through whom they paid their revenue to Government. The writings last referred to are called *pottahs*, and, though they are here and elsewhere in the Regulations treated as leases, yet they do not represent any particular transaction, and therefore admit of being restricted to terms of years, or enlarged into estates of inheritance, according to the phraseology employed. Of the last description of pottahs are the pottahs to Talookdars, 'whose tenure is denominated *Junglebooree*,' and who were not considered entitled to separation from the proprietors of whom they held. 'The pottahs granted to these Talookdars, in consideration of the grantee clearing away the jungle and bringing the land into a productive state, give it to him and his heirs in perpetuity, exempting him from payment of revenue for a certain term, and at the expiration of it subjecting him to a certain specific *asul jumma* for such part of the land only as the grantee brings into a state of cultivation.' 'The pottah specifies the boundaries of the land granted, but not the quantity of land until it is brought into cultivation.'

Pottahs described.

Jungle-boorce tenures.

Under the category of Independent Talooks were included tenures called *Malgoozary Aymas*. *Ayma*, or more correctly *Aimma*, is the plural of the word *Imam*, which is applied to the leader at the devotions of an assembly of private worshippers, as well as to the head of the Mohammedan community. *Ayma* tenures were grants of land to Imams by Mohammedan sovereigns, and were sometimes entirely free from the payment of revenue, but sometimes subject to a fixed rent. The former

Malgoozary Aymas.

were included in the *Seyurghal* already mentioned, and will meet us again when we come to the *La Khiraj* tenures; the latter were the *Malgoozary Aymas* just mentioned. These were to be separated from the proprietors to whom their revenue was paid, as coming under the rules for the separation of Talookdars, who are the proprietors of the lands comprising their Talooks. *Malgoozary Ayma* tenures were, however, sometimes granted for the purpose of bringing waste lands into cultivation; and these were classed with Dependent Talooks, as coming within the rules respecting the *Junglebooree* Talooks, already mentioned. Some other tenures are mentioned in the Regulation in connection with the settlement of the revenue, but any further notice of these would be superfluous in this place.

After the settlement of the revenue was concluded with the Independent Talookdars, there would no longer be any occasion for the distinction between Dependent and Independent Talookdars, for the latter would become, in fact, Zemindars, and the subordinate condition of the former would be sufficiently indicated by the name Talookdar, which means literally the holder of a dependency.

Value of proprietary rights in the soil according to the Government estimate.

Though the Zemindars and Independent Talookdars were dealt with for the purposes of the settlement as the actual proprietors of the soil, it does not appear, from the terms that were granted to them, that the Government of the time entertained any very exalted ideas of their proprietary rights.

Previous to the Decennial settlement, settlements for shorter periods had been made in many instances with the Zemindars, and in fixing the new assessment, the *jumma* of the preceding year was taken with some modifications as the standard. But that standard 'could not be applied to the separated Talooks which had not theretofore paid any *jumma* immediately to the Government'; nor was it understood to be applicable 'to any instances where the actual produce of the land had been ascertained.' In all such instances the assessment was to be regulated so as to leave to the proprietors a provision for themselves and families equal to about ten per cent. on the amount of their contributions to Government, including the produce of their *nankar* or other private lands to be annexed to the *Malgoozary* lands.' Ten per cent. on the contributions is one-eleventh of the whole amount contributed, and if we can ascertain the relation of the amount to the whole produce of the land, we shall have some measure of the value put on the Zemindar's proprietary rights. According to the Mohammedan law, a half of the produce of the land was the extreme limit of what could properly be taken from the cultivator, and that was believed by Mr. Shore to be the actual proportion in which the ryots were taxed in Bengal,[1] so that one-twenty-second part of the whole produce of the land was about the estimate of the value of the proprietary rights of the Zemindar, put upon them by the Government at the time of the perpetual settlement of the revenue in Bengal;—rather a slender foundation, it must be allowed, for the superstructure of subsidiary rights that was supposed to rest upon it.

Powers over the ryots possessed by and conferred in the Zemindars and other assumed proprietors.

The Zemindars and other landholders were supposed to have the power of summoning, and if necessary, compelling the attendance of their tenants, for the adjustment of their rents, or for any other just purpose, and of measuring any land within their respective estates which may be liable to measurement.[2] So also they were held to be entitled to the unoccupied or waste land within their Zemindaries; for *jungle boorie* pottahs granted by them in consideration of the grantees' clearing away the jungle and bringing the land into a productive estate were recognised as valid, and quite within their power to grant. Now, the power to measure the land was a sovereign right, exercised, as we have seen, by Ala-ood-deen, and on a larger scale by Akbar, and repeated by his successors on three several occasions in Bengal, when additions were made to the *Asul Toomar jummah.* So also it was the sovereign, as representative of the Imam, who had the sole right to authorise the cultivation and appro-

[1] Ap. F. R. p. 184.

[2] See Reg. vii. of 1799, § 13, cl. 8, where the powers are confirmed.

priation of wastes. It seems, therefore, probable that if the rights referred to were possessed by the Zemindars at the time of the perpetual settlement of the revenue, it was not by virtue of any proprietary rights of their own, but as *Amils* or collectors of the public revenue, under the *Sunnuds*, which directed them among other things 'to encourage the body of ryots in such a manner that signs of an increased cultivation and improvement of the country may duly appear.' Be that as it may, these powers were supposed to be possessed by the Zemindars and independent Talookdars, and an important addition was made to them by another Regulation passed at the same time,[1] which empowered 'the Zemindars, Independent Talookdars, and other actual proprietors of land, to distrain the crops and products of the earth of every description, the grown cattle and all other personal property belonging to their under-farmers and ryots, for arrears of rent and revenue, and to cause the said property to be sold for the discharge of such arrears.' It is of importance to observe that the same power of distress was vested in Dependent Talookdars for the recovery of the arrears of rent from their under-farmers and ryots; and as the other powers of compelling the attendance of ryots, and of measuring the land, were assumed to belong not only to the Zemindars but to 'other landholders,' a term which would comprehend the Dependent Talookdars, it would seem to have been the intention of Government to place them in all respects in the same relative position to the ryots as the Zemindars were in to themselves.

Effect of the settlement on the condition of the Zemindars and ryots.

The effect, then, of the permanent settlement on the condition of the Zemindars and ryots, was to raise the former from the condition of *Amils* or collectors of the public revenue, and to establish them permanently as proprietors of the land, between the Government and the *Khoodkasht* ryots, while it reduced the latter from the condition of proprietors, or at least tenants in chief of the sovereign, which their predecessors the *Wuzeefa* holders

[1] R. xvii. of 1793, § 2.

are shown to have been under Akbar and Aurungzebe, to that of tenants of the Zemindars; and not only so, but also in some cases to establish permanently, between the Zemindars and ryots, a class of sub-proprietors under the name of Talookdars. It seems to have been the original intention of the Government that this class of sub-proprietors should not be allowed to increase, for the Zemindars were prevented from creating any more tenures of that kind, by restricting their power of granting leases to ten years. But that restriction was removed by Regulation V. of 1812, and by a subsequent Regulation (VII. of 1819) they were not only empowered to multiply talooks indefinitely, but the same power was committed to the Talookdars of creating similar tenures to hold of themselves. So that we have now not only *Putny Talookdars*, as the first are called, holding of the Zemindars, but *dur-putny dars*, holding similarly of the *putny dars*, and *se-putny dars*, holding in the same manner of the *dur-putny dars*; with a tendency to a further extension downwards, and also laterally, through all the Zillahs of Bengal.[1]

Putny Talookdars.

It was foreseen that the large powers assumed to be possessed by the Zemindars and Talookdars, or now conferred on them, might be abused to the detriment of the ryots, and certain provisions were made for their protection. With regard to some part of the lands, the custom prevailed of varying the rents as the *Khiraj* was originally varied, according to the different kinds of produce. In other places the whole had been converted into one lump sum called the *Asul*, or original of the *Toomar jummah.* This had been raised on three different occasions in Bengal, as already mentioned, and subsequently to the last of these, various additions had been made to it by the local Governments or by the Zemindars under the name of *Abwab*. Some of these *Abwab* were added to the *Asul*, but the power of making any further exactions of the same kind was expressly taken away from the

[1] Preamble to last Regulation.

Zemindars. All that could be done with regard to the other lands, was to refer them to the *nirikh-bundee*, or supposed custom of the Pergunnah; and as no means were ever taken to ascertain what the *nirikh* was, the ryots were left very much at the mercy of the Zemindars, and became thus ultimately reduced to a condition not far removed from that of tenants at will.

La Khiraj tenures.

IV. I have already shown that all appropriations of the *Khiraj*, or land revenue, extending beyond the life of the grantee, were absolutely void by the Mohammedan law.[1] But the British Government in its liberality, determined that 'all grants for holding land exempt from the payment of revenue made previous to the Company's accession to the Dewanny, by whatever authority, and whether by a writing or without a writing, should be deemed valid, provided the grantee actually and *boná fide* obtained possession of the land so granted previous to the date above mentioned.' The only authority by which such grants could have been lawfully made was the *Badshah*, or king; but 'numerous grants of this description were made, not only by the Zemindars, but by the officers of Government appointed to the temporary superintendence of the collection of the revenue, under the pretext that the produce of the land was to be applied to religious or charitable purposes.' Grants emanating from the sovereign were termed 'Badshahee,' the others 'not Badshahee'; and provisions were made for both kinds of grants separately by Regulations XIX. and XXXVII. of 1793. In both of these the provision before mentioned was contained; and it was also declared in both that all grants of either kind for holding lands exempt from the payment of revenue that might have been made since the 12th of August, 1765, by any other authority than that of Government, and which might not have been confirmed by Government, or any officer authorised to confirm them, were invalid. There was no power to make *Badshahee*

Divided into Badshahee, and non-Badshahee.

[1] See *ante*, p. xxiv.; and Ap. F. R. p. 318.

grants in the Lower Provinces after that date; but the manufacture of the *non-Badshahee* seems to have gone on as before, and a distinction was therefore drawn between such of them, on the one hand, as had been made between the 12th of August, 1765, and the 1st of December, 1790; and those of them, on the other, that were made subsequent to the latter date. The former were only to be invalid as regards the Government revenue, and no more than half the usual revenue was to be assessed upon them; while, with regard to the latter, they were declared to be null and void, and no length of possession was to give validity to such grants, 'either with regard to the property in the soil or the rents of it.'

Though all grants on which possession had been obtained before the 1st of August, 1765, were declared to be valid for the life of the original grantee, no grant of either description was to exempt the lands from revenue after his death, where the grant expressly specified it to have been given for the life of the grantee; or, supposing that there was no writing, or the writing for the grant did not specify whether it was to be considered hereditary or otherwise, when the grant, from the nature or denomination of it, should be proved to be 'a life tenure only,' 'according to the ancient usages of the country.' Where, again, there was no such evidence of a life tenure, then a distinction was made between the Badshahee and non-Badshahee grants. The former, with the exception of the Jaghire, were assumed to be hereditary unless proved to be the contrary; while the latter were not to be considered hereditary unless proved to be so from their nature and denomination, according to the ancient usages of the country.[1]

In both Regulations it will be seen that exemption from revenue is sometimes treated as a personal right, limited to the life of the grantee, and sometimes as a quality adhering to the land, and capable of being hereditary. This is not agreeable to Mohammedan law, ac-

[1] Reg. xix. and xxxvii. of 1793, § 2, cl. 4 of both.

cording to which all land that is not *Ooshree* is *Khirajee* and even when the owner is excused from the payment of the *Khiraj*, the land cannot be said to be exempted from it; for its character as *Khirajee* still remains, though the owner is temporarily allowed to appropriate the *Khiraj* to himself.

Non-Badshahee grants.

Of *non-Badshahee* grants, the following are, I think, generally allowed to be by their nature and denomination *La Khiraj*, and hereditary according to the usages of the country: 1st. Bermooter or land granted to Brahmins for the support of themselves and descendants. 2nd. Bishnpareet, or land granted to religious persons professing the special service of the Deity Vishnu. 3rd. Deotur, or land granted for the support of a temple or idol. 4th. Mohuteran, or land assigned generally to religious persons, or for religious purposes. 5th. Bustomitter, or land granted to Bustoms, or Hindoo religious mendicants; and 6th. Fakeeran, or lands granted to Fakeers, or Mohammedan religious mendicants. All these, it will be seen, are for religious or charitable uses, and are at the present time included in the accounts of the Bengal Zemindars, under the head of *Mujara-een*, or lands that have been assigned away as an allowance, and which consequently do not pay revenue.'[1]

Badshahee grants.

With regard to Badshahee grants, the following are mentioned in Regulation XXXVII. of 1793, § 2, namely, Altumgah, Jaghire, Ayma, and Mududmash; and they are all described as 'Grants for holding lands exempt from the payment of revenue.' By a subsequent section it is declared that 'Altumgah, Ayma, and Mududmash grants are to be considered hereditary,' but Jaghires are to be considered as life tenures, and, with all other life tenures, are to expire with the life of the grantee, unless otherwise expressed in the grant. From this it would appear that, in the view of the framers of the Regulation the Jaghire was, like the other Badshahee grants, a tenure of land, and differed from them only that,

Jaghire.

[1] Smith's *Zumeendaree Accounts, passim.*

while the others were hereditary, the Jaghire was usually for life, though it might also be made hereditary by words to that effect in the grant. That this is not a correct description of the Jaghire may, I think, be inferred from what has been said of the origin and progress of that kind of grant. But to make the matter more clear, let us revert a little more particularly to the examples of unconditional Jaghires that have been already referred to in this essay, namely the Jaghire to Lord Clive, and the forms Nos. II. and III. in the Appendix. For the better understanding of the first it is to be observed that the Zemindary of Calcutta, or the 24 Pergunnahs, had been previously granted to the East India Company, subject to an annual payment of sicca rupees 222,958, to the Royal treasury, and that the dignity of a *Munsubdar* of the Empire had been conferred on Lord Clive. To support that dignity a *Jaghire* of the above sum was appointed to him, without any limitation in respect of time; so that it would remain to him for his life. It was afterwards restricted to ten years, with a grant of the reversion to the East India Company by a firman reciting that the sum of sicca rupees 222,958 and odd had 'been appropriated from the aforesaid payments as an unconditional Jaghire to the high and mighty Lord Clive,' and then declaring that the same 'are confirmed,' and 'shall appertain as an unconditional Jaghire to the high and mighty aforesaid' for ten years from a date mentioned, after which 'they shall revert as an unconditional Jaghire to the Company.' The other two forms above referred to are to the same effect. In both of them a sum of money, so many *lakhs* of *daums*, is said to be bestowed on a particular individual out of the revenues of a specified Pergunnah, by way of Jageer, and, like the Jaghire to Lord Clive, both the forms contain a requisition to the persons by whom the revenue is payable, to account for it to the Jageerdar. Without something of this kind, which is equivalent to the appointment of him as an agent, it is difficult to conceive how the Jageer could be made available in any way known to the Mohammedan law. As a debt due, or to become due, it could not in strictness be the subject of a gift to any but the debtor. When given to him, being an extinction of the debt, it might without much impropriety be said to be granted in perpetuity, as in the case of the reversion of Lord Clive's Jageer to the East India Company, who were debtors in that amount to the Mogul Government. But in the case of any other person than the debtor, the only way in which a debt could be transferred was by making the transferee the agent of the original creditor;[1] or, what is the same thing, requiring the debtor to pay it to him. But an appointment of agency does not pass at the death of the agent to his heir, but is *ipso facto* cancelled.[2] So that it is difficult to imagine how a Jaghire, in the strict and proper sense of the term, could be made hereditary. Indeed, so established had its character as a life estate become in the usages of the country, that in a case decided in the Sudder Dewany Adaulut of Calcutta (Reports, Vol. II. p. 191), it was held to be a good ground, among others, for suspecting the genuineness of a Sunnud granting a Jaghire, that it contained a condition that it should be hereditary.

Altumgha. Of the Altumgha I have already said enough, and will only observe in this place that the grant mentioned under that name in the Regulation, which is said to be hereditary in its own nature, is not a grant of revenue, but a grant of land exempt from the payment of revenue. Though we sometimes hear of an Altumgha Jageer, I think it will always be found to mean a grant of land exempt from the payment of revenue. It is true that the Altumgha grant of the Dewany to the East India Company, which was in reality a Jaghire, was intended to be perpetual; yet it could only become so, as already observed, by the sufferance of the grantor's royal successors; and accordingly we find that the firman contained a request to them to 'leave the said office in the possession

[1] *Digest*, p. 522. [2] *Hidayah*, vol. iv. p. 231.

of the said Company from generation to generation for ever.'

Ayma Mudud-mash.

With regard to the remaining Badshahee grants mentioned in the Regulation, enough has been said of the Ayma when speaking of Malgoozary Aymas; but a few words are required in elucidation of the mudud-mash, on account of the words 'and posterity,' which are found in one of the examples (No. I.) in the Appendix; the original being *furzundan* or children; a word which frequently occurs in modern deeds, and even in deeds by Hindoos, though it is one of the Mohammedan law. *Mudud* means assistance, and the grant is essentially the same as that mentioned in the *Ayeen Akbery*, and before referred to under the name of *mudd-ul-mash*. In English law a distinction is made between the transfer of personal property and the transfer of real property, and a sale or gift of the latter can be effected only by a writing, which expresses that it is made to the purchaser or donee 'and his heirs'; as without the latter words an estate for life only would be conveyed to him. No such distinctions exist in the Mohammedan law. Sale or gift of real as of personal property may be made verbally; and in either case there is a complete transfer of the whole estate of the seller or donor to the purchaser or donee. The *Bei-nameh* (deed of sale), *heba nameh* (deed of gift), or *tumleek nameh*, applicable to both, is only evidence of the transaction; and the addition of the words 'and heirs,' or the like, when they have any meaning at all, is to restrict rather than to enlarge the estate conveyed. The words 'and heirs' would be entirely nugatory, as no living person can have heirs, these being indeterminable till his death. But if the words were 'and children,' and there were any persons at the time in existence to whom the words could be properly applied, the sale or gift would be to the purchaser or donee and his children jointly. It could not be to them *after* him, for that would reduce his estate to one for life, which would be inconsistent with the nature of sale or gift; and, in order

Meaning of the word children (*Furzundan*) in the latter grant.

to give the words any meaning at all they must be taken to convey a joint estate, in the same way as if any other person than his children were conjoined with him. If there were no persons answering to the description of his children in existence at the time, the words would be nugatory, and the sale or gift would be to the purchaser or donee alone. But the word *furzundan* is not restricted to children of the loins. It has a technical meaning, which it is now necessary to explain. In the first place it means children of the loins without any distinction of sex. In the next generation it comprehends the children of sons in the same way without distinction of sex, and so on in the following generations, females being included in each, but their children excluded in the next. So long as there are children in any generation the next is excluded. So that a mudud-mash grant to a man and his children, is to him and the sons and daughters of his loins if there are any living at the time; if there are none, then it is to him and the sons and daughters of his sons if there be any, and so on. While, if there are none to whom the name of children can be properly applied, the grant is to him alone. It will be observed that children unborn are in no case included, and to give them any interest in the produce of an estate it is necessary to throw it into *wukf* or settlement. A gift being in its nature absolute, or what is called in English law a fee simple, any restriction of its enjoyment or of the power to alienate it would be void as being inconsistent with its essential character. So that a thing cannot be given for life.[1] Its produce, however, may be reserved for successive generations when the thing itself is put into *wukf* or settlement. In these circumstances the same construction is I think to be put on the word children (*furzundan*) as that above assigned to it, though it has become usual, for more certainty perhaps, to add after the word *furzundan*, the phrase *butnun baad butn*, or generation after generation, and sometimes (indeed commonly) with

[1] *Digest*, p. 509.

the further addition of *nuslun baad nusl*. *Butn* means literally *venter*, and the first expression does no more than serve simply to convey the idea that the generations, if more than one, are not to be taken *pari passu*, but in succession. *Nusl*, however, has a precise meaning of its own, which may enlarge the meaning of *furzundan* when added to it; for if one should make a settlement on his *nusl*, the children of his sons and the children of his daughters would be included whether near or remote.[1]

Ghatwallee tenures.

Nearly allied to the Lakhiraj tenures is another tenure called *Ghatwallee*, which, though perhaps older and more genuine than many of them, has not been fully brought to light till our own times. The word *Ghatwallee* is a compound of *Ghat*, a pass or ferry, *wallah*, a keeper, and *ee*, a relative particle, so that the whole word means literally, something relating to a *Ghat*-keeper, the person being the principal object of consideration, as in all cases of the application of the *Khiraj*. 'Securing the passes' is expressly included among the purposes to which the *Khiraj* may be applied, and a *Ghatwallah* is thus strictly one of the *Ahl Khiraj*. The practice of appointing special persons to guard the passes seems to have originated in Beerbhoom, which is described by Mr. James Grant[2] as 'the largest Mussulman Zemindary in Bengal,' and as having been 'conferred by Jaffier Khan on Assid Ullah, of the Afghan or Patan tribe, for the political purpose of guarding the frontiers against the incursions of the barbarous Hindoos of Jharcund.' Mr. Grant further remarks that the tenure on which the district was held, 'corresponded in some respects with the ancient military fiefs of Europe, inasmuch as certain lands were held *lakhiraje*, or exempted from the payment of revenue, and to be solely appropriated to the maintenance of troops.' There is no doubt (according to a high authority), 'that the tenures here spoken of are *Ghatwallee* tenures, though they are not mentioned by that name.' This remark occurs in the judgment of the Privy Council in the case of

[1] *Fut Al.* as quoted in *Digest*, p. 572. [2] Ap. F. R. p. 268.

'Rajah Lelalund Singh, Appellant, *v.* The Government of Bengal, Respondents.'[1] The suit was originally brought by the Government against Toofany Sing Ghatwal, for resumption of the revenue on his lands, and the Rajah, being allowed to intervene, became the principal defendant in the suit. A decree was pronounced in favour of the Government by the special commissioner, 'who ordered the land to be resumed, and assessed under clause 4 section 8 of Regulation I. of 1793, as being granted for police establishments;' and an appeal having been preferred to Her Majesty in Council, this became 'the great question in the suit.' But the judgment was reversed on the 15th of June, 1855, on the ground that 'the lands are not properly under the meaning of the clause relied on by the Respondent; that they were a part of the Zemindary of Khurruckpore, and were included in the settlement for the Zemindary, and covered by the *jumma* assessed upon it.' With regard to the tenure their Lordships remarked that, 'though the nature and extent of the right of the Ghatwal in the Ghatwallee villages may be doubtful, there clearly was some ancient law or usage by which the lands were appropriated to reward the services of the Ghatwals; services which, though they would include the performance of duties of police, were quite as much in their origin of a military as of a civil character, and would require the appointment of a different class of persons from ordinary police officers.' I have noticed in an early part of this essay, that, in disposing of the lands of a conquered country, the Imam may, if he pleases, reserve them by way of *wukf*, or as an appropriation for the purposes of war. Khurruckpore is adjacent to Beerbhoom, and it is natural to suppose that Jaffier Khan, when he was making his arrangements for the latter district, and had to appoint a Zemindar for Khurruckpore, would not have left it exposed to the same tribes of marauders on its frontier, but would set apart some of its lands for the purpose of securing the passes against

[1] Moore's *Indian Appeals*, vol. vi. p. 466.

their inroads. Inquiry on that subject was not deemed necessary for the decision of the matter before the Court; and accordingly all that was decided was, that the Government was prevented from resuming the lands because they had been included in the settlement with the Zemindar. But let us suppose that some such appropriation had been made as conjectured by the Judicial Committee of the Privy Council, that is, by way of *wukf*, the only way recognised by the Mohammedan law. The legal effects of such a measure would be to render the lands of the villages inalienable for ever, and to restrict the application of their produce to the purposes designated so long as they were capable of being fulfilled. All that would remain to the appropriator in such circumstances would be the right to appoint from time to time proper persons to carry into effect the purposes of the appropriation. This right would pass, by the transfer of the Dewany, to the East India Company; and it is all that could pass or be transferred by them to the Zemindar of Khurruckpore, by including the lands in his Zemindary at the time of the perpetual settlement of the revenue; so that, if there ever was an actual appropriation of the land, as is highly probable, its produce could never be lawfully diverted from the purposes originally designated, and neither the Government nor the Zemindar would have any power to resume the revenue of the land, though each were entirely unembarrassed by the rights of the other: not even, though the purposes should in the course of time happen to fail; for then, according to Aboo Yoosuf, whose opinion has been generally adopted, the produce must be applied for the benefit of the poor.

It is only land that there is any authority for saying that the Imam could reserve, by way of *wukf* for warlike purposes. If the land were disposed of, as, for instance, if it were in the possession of ryots, or cultivators, all that would remain to the Government would be the revenue, which could be made directly available for warlike or other purposes, only by *tunkhas*, or assignments, directed to the persons by whom it was payable; in other words, by granting *jageers*, which, if burdened with services to be performed, as in the case of the *ghatwals*, would be conditional. If the *jageers* were renewed when they became vacant, the tenure of any existing *ghatwal* would present the same appearance as if the land had been originally appropriated to *ghatwallee* purposes. But then the grantor would be under no obligation to renew, and might, on the occurrence of a vacancy, resume the revenue for any other purpose to which the *khiraj* was applicable; which he would be precluded from doing if there ever had been any special appropriation. These remarks will prepare us for the consideration of another class of *ghatwallee* cases more recently disposed of in the Privy Council, by the decision in what was taken as the ruling case of the whole, namely, the case of Rajah Nilmoney Singh, Appellant, *v.* The Government of Bengal and Beer Singh, Respondents. The suit was originally brought by the Rajah against Beer Singh for the resumption of certain villages, on the ground that the plaintiff's ancestor gave them to the defendants' ancestor, in lieu of pay for personal services to be rendered to the Pachete Zemindars, which were no longer required. The Government put in a claim on the ground that the villages constituted a *jageer mehal* for the payment of police services, and that the Plaintiff could not resume the lands so long as Government required the services to be rendered. This, it will be seen hereafter, became the main point in the case, and the only one that was decided by the judgment. But Beer Singh himself merely stated in his Answer that the disputed villages were his ancestral *jageer*. The true nature of the *jageer*, however, came out in the statements of third parties, who claimed to have some interest in them. From these statements it appeared that the villages formed the *jageer* lands of Ghat Dhekea, of which Beer Singh was only the *sirdar*, or head *jageerdar*, having subordinates under him (including the claimants) who were called *tabehdars*; and these facts were confirmed by Beer Singh's witnesses, and indeed admitted by himself, when called upon as a witness on behalf of Government. He then declared that the *jageer* lands of Ghat Dhekea had been given to his ancestor in order to protect the *ghat*, and that, in fact, he and the other *jageerdars* against whom similar suits were brought by the same plaintiff, 'are Government Ghatwals.' In these circumstances the Plaintiff filed, as evidence in the suit, the copy of an old sunnud given to the ancestor of another *jageerdar*, but said to be applicable to the *jageers* in all the cases. It was in the following terms: 'To Mohagur Singh of good manners. It is written that in the Pergunnah of Khaspaille, there is a jummah of yours, in the village of Bitrajore, a former jageer. Having confirmed this, you are appointed to the office. Divide the rent of the mouzahs in the year 1176 into two parts. Taking possession of one share of the *jageer*, you shall remain in the performance of the service with your brothers. If you do anything to the contrary the jageer will be resumed. Dated the 7th Assar, 1177. The end. The 18th June' (1780). The sunnud bore the seal of a British officer, as well as the signature of the Zemindar, and, as Zemindars at that time were only officers of the Government, it is evident that it must have been granted by the governing power of the time. Now, as regards the contents of the sunnud, it will be remembered that *jummah* is the proper subject of a *jageer*, and, as it came out in evidence that the lands were in the possession of ryots, it is evident that all which could be received by the ghatwals was the *jummah*, or revenue, payable by them; and that, therefore, the *ghatwallee* tenure in this and the other cases was, not merely in name but in substance also, a conditional *jageer*. The main question, however, in the suit was that raised by the Government, as already mentioned, and it was accordingly that only that was decided. The suit was dismissed on the ground that the plaintiff could not resume the lands so long as Government required the services to be rendered, and the judgment was confirmed on the same grounds on appeal. A special appeal was then preferred to the High Court of Calcutta, and, that Court being bound by the concurrent judgments of the Courts below, the appeal was dismissed, and the judgment was confirmed on a further appeal to the Privy Council. The question how the lands were settled at the Decennial settlement was deemed immaterial by the judge of first instance, because, being devoted and held subject to service rendered to Government, 'the Zemindar could not resume unless the Government waived its right.' This may be thought to imply that, in the opinion of the judge, the Zemindar would not be precluded from resuming the lands if the Government should ever think proper to waive its claim. The lands were liable to what was called a *punchukee*, or low rent, and the real object of the Zemindar was to raise it by re-assessment up to the full amount of a proper *jummah*. It did not appear when this rent was imposed on the land, but let us suppose that it existed at the time of the decennial settlement, and had been taken into account in fixing the revenue of the Zemindary, still a part of the *jummah* was in *jageer*, and the land *pro tanto lakhiraj*. But by § 36 Reg. VIII. of 1793, 'all existing *lakherage* lands' were expressly excluded from the settlement, 'whether exempted from the kherage (or public revenue) with or without due authority.' It is difficult, therefore, to conceive how the Zemindar could have any right to that part of the jummah which was in *jageer*, even though the Government should waive its claim to the service; in other words, how he should ever be able to raise the rent above the *punchukee* to which it was already liable.

In the case of the *ghatwals* of Khurruckpore, the Government was prevented from resuming the revenue of the lands because they had been included in the settlement with the Zemindar. That objection would not apply to the *ghatwallee jageers* in Pachete; and it would seem that the Government, being under no obligation to keep up the *jageers*, might resume the revenue of the land so far as it had been in *jageer*, at any time on the occurrence of a vacancy. They might, however, be restrained by equitable considerations arising out of circumstances not fully developed in the proceedings of the case before the Court.

In the case of the Khurruckpore *ghatwals*, the tenure is supposed to have originated in a special appropriation of the land. In that of the Pachete *ghatwals* the tenure was evidently a conditional jageer. But it appeared from the copy of the old sunnud, and other evidence in the case of Beer Singh, that appointments to the office whenever it became vacant were usually made in the same family; until at length the leading member of the family seems to have assumed the office on a vacancy without waiting for a formal appointment from the superior authority. Thus, Beroo Singh, the grandfather of Beer Singh, was succeeded by his son, Pochum Singh, he by his son, Roop Singh, and he by his infant son Chundy Churn Singh, for whom his uncle, Beer Singh, continued to manage the *ghatwallee* for several years, and it was not till his death that Beer Singh became the *jageerdar*. Long before this the *Ghatwallee* tenure had become hereditary in Beerbhoom, where, as already mentioned, it seems to have originated; for in the preamble to Regulation XXIX. of 1814, 'this class of persons' (meaning the *ghatwals*) are said to be 'entitled to hold their lands generation after generation in perpetuity; subject, nevertheless, to an established and fixed rent to the Zemindar of Beerbhoom, and to the performance of certain duties for the maintenance of the public peace and support of the police.' The Regulation being silent as to any division of the lands between co-sharers, or the heirs of a deceased *ghatwal*, a suit was brought in the Zillah Court of Beerbhoom by Hurlal Singh, one of three sharers, against his co-sharers for a regular *butwara* or division of the mehal, and separate possession of the share belonging to him. The judge decreed that the several shareholders should hold joint possession, and that the profits, after the payment of necessary expenses, should be divided amongst the several partners in proportion to their respective shares. A special appeal having been preferred to the Sudder Dewany Adawlut of Calcutta, the judge before whom it first came for decision, referred the point whether such property came under the Hindoo rules of inheritance, and might be divided among the coparceners, to the opinion of his colleagues; and out of six judges of which the Court was composed, five were of opinion that the mehal could not be divided. The question was put with reference to the nature of the *ghatwallee* mehals generally, and the single judge who differed from his colleagues was of opinion that the question should be decided by local usage. The judge who referred the case then gave his decision 'that a mehal of this nature cannot be divided, but should on the death of an incumbent devolve entirely on the eldest son or the next ghatwal;' and another judge having concurred with him, the judgment became final. (Reports, vol. vi. p. 171.) The first part of the judgment, having reference to the general nature of *ghatwallee* lands, is a precedent on the point that lands of that kind cannot be divided wherever they may happen to be situated. But the question of succession to such lands was not properly before the Court, and the latter part of the judgment ought, perhaps, to be considered as only an *obiter dictum* of the two judges. It seems also doubtful whether they thought that the succession to the land should follow that of the *ghatwallee*, or *vice versa*. The former meaning seems to be more congenial to the origin and history of the *ghatwallee* tenure, particularly when the duties to it were more exclusively of a military character, and required the selection of better qualified persons for their performance. Afterwards, when the duties sunk into those of mere police, which almost any person was qualified to perform, the power of selection may have fallen into abeyance, and then the succession to the office would more naturally follow that of the land. Usage seems to have been tending in that direction in the case of the Pachete jageerdars; and on the whole, usage may, perhaps, be the safest guide in cases to which the last-mentioned precedent may not be considered to be strictly applicable.

THE LAND TAX OF INDIA,

ACCORDING TO THE MOOHUMMUDAN LAW.

THE

LAND TAX OF INDIA.

CHAPTER I.

OF OOSHR[1] AND KHIRAJ,[2] OR TITHE AND TRIBUTE.

[This Chapter is taken from the *Futawa Alumgeeree*, vol. ii. p. 337.]

LANDS are of two kinds, *Ooshree* and *Khirajee;* and the whole land of Arabia, which comprehends the lands of Tehama, Hejaz, Mecca, Yemen, Taif, Ooman, and Bahrein, is *Ooshree.*[3] Moohummud has said that the land of Arabia extends from Azeeb to Mecca, and from Aden Abein to the remotest coast of Yemen, in Mehrah, and that with regard to the *Sowad*[4] of Irak, so much of it as is watered by *Ajumee,*[5] canals, is *Khirajee.* The Sowad extends in

Ooshree and Khirajee Land. Arabia is Ooshree.

The Sowad

[1] Literally a *tenth part.*

[2] Pronounced also *Khuraj.* It means literally *going out,* and is applied in law to tribute, as an "outgoing" from the produce of the earth. *Inayah*, vol. ii. p. 587.

[3] Because neither the Prophet nor any of his four orthodox successors, imposed the *Khiraj* on that country. *Hidayah*, vol. ii. p. 775; *Translation*, vol. ii. p. 204.

[4] Literally *blackness.* It is applied to the villages of Irak, from the dark green colour of their trees and crops. *Kifayah*, vol. ii. p. 774.

[5] Persian, but more generally every people not Arabian.

B

of Irak is Khirajee.

length from the boundaries of Mowsul to the land of Abadden, and in breadth from the termination of the mountains in the land of Hulwan to the remotest part of Kadseea, near to Azeeb in the territory of Arabia. Every country besides these, which was forcibly subdued and bestowed on its inhabitants, without their embracing the faith of *Islam*, is *Khirajee* (if connected with *Khiraj* water[1]); and every country which was peaceably subdued by submitting to the *jizyut*,[2] is also *Khiraj* land. But every country forcibly subdued and divided by the Imam among the soldiers,[3] is *Ooshree*. While every country forcibly subdued, the inhabitants of which embraced the faith before the Imam had passed any order with regard to them, was at his discretion, and might be divided among the soldiers, whereupon it would have become *Ooshree;* or if he pleased, he might have bestowed it upon the inhabitants, and after the bestowal he would still have had the option of imposing the *Ooshr* upon it, or the *Khiraj* if it were watered by *Khiraj* water. (*Futawa Kazee Khan*).

Rules as to other countries.

Every land, the people of which voluntarily embrace the faith, is *Ooshree.* And in this manner the whole land of Arabia, when it was subdued by force and violence, and its inhabitants, from being worshippers of idols, were converted to the faith, and the Imam gave up their lands to them, became *Ooshree.*[4] So, also, every country of the nations of *Ajum*,[5] with regard to which, when the Imam conquered it, he hesitated whether he should grant the people their lives and lands, and impose on the latter the *Khiraj*, or should divide it among the soldiers, and impose

[1] Briefly explained in the next chapter, but more fully in the introduction.

[2] Capitation tax. Submission to it implies submission to *Khiraj* also, which is sometimes called the *jizyut* of land.

[3] Arab. *Ghanimeen*, persons entitled to the plunder, from *ghuneemut*, booty.

[4] The fact is, that idolatry was not tolerated in Arabia, and the greater part of its inhabitants being idolaters, had no alternative but to embrace the faith.

[5] That is, every country but Arabia.

the *Ooshr* on the land, and then said, "I have made their lands *Ooshree*," and began to do so, but subsequently granted the people their lives and lands, remains *Ooshree*. This Moohummud has stated in the Nuwadir, and Kurkhee in his book. And in like manner, *Khiraj* land, when cut off from the supply of *Khiraj* water, and watered with *Ooshr* water, is *Ooshree*.[1] (*Moheet.*)

Waste Lands, how to be assessed when brought into cultivation.

When a person has brought waste land into cultivation, if it be contiguous to *Khirajee* land, it is *Khirajee*, and if it be contiguous to *Ooshree* land, it is *Ooshree*.[2] But this, only, when the person who brought it into cultivation was a Mooslim; for if he were a *Zimmee*,[3] the land would be *Khirajee*, even though it should be contiguous to *Ooshree* land. Bussorah is *Ooshree* by the general agreement of the companions.[4] (*Siraj-ool-wuhhaj.*)

Khiraj is of two kinds, *Mookasimah* and *Wuzeefa*.

The *Khiraj* of lands is of two kinds; *Mookasimah*,[5] which is something out of the produce, as a fifth or sixth, or the like; and *Wuzeefa*,[6] which is something in obligation,[7] and dependent on the return that the land is capable of yielding. (*Futawa Kazee Khan*). The *Mookasimah Khiraj* depends on the actual crop or issue from the land, not on the kind of crop which it is capable of bearing; insomuch that, like the *Ooshr*, it is not due when the land, though capable, is allowed to lie idle. (*Tatar Khaneeah*, taken from the *Zukheerah.*) But as to the *Wuzeefa Khiraj*,

Rate of *Wuzeefa*.

[1] It is implied, I think, that the land belongs to a Mooslim.

[2] Moohummud differed from Aboo Huneefa and Aboo Yoosuf on this point, according to his principle, that the impost is regulated by the nature of the water. *Hamilton's Hedaya*, vol. ii. p. 207.

[3] Subject of a *Mooslim* power, but of a different religion.

[4] From its contiguity to the Sowad it would otherwise have been *Khirajee*.

[5] Mutual division; from *kismut*, division or partition.

[6] Also called *moowuzzuf*, both words being inflexions of the same root, and signifying *fixed* or *agreed upon*.

[7] Indeterminate, as existing only in the obligation of the person who is bound to render it. See *Moohummudan Law of Sale*, (*Baillie*), Introduction, p. 45.

Moohummud has said that it is a *kufeez* and a *dirhem*[1] on every *jureeb* of land fit for sowing, and five *dirhems* for a *jureeb* of vegetables,[2] and ten dirhems for a jureeb of orchards.[3] (*Moheet.*) And on other kinds, such as saffron cotton, gardens, &c., an imposition will be laid according to their capability, the extreme of capability being a half of the produce as the amount of duty. A garden[4] is any land enclosed with a wall, and planted with different kinds of palms, vines, and other trees, so wide apart that the ground between them admits of being cultivated; and if the trees be so closely planted or entangled that the ground between them cannot be cultivated, the place is called an orchard.[5] (*Kafee.*)

[1] A foreign word, though naturalized in the Arabic language. Evidently the Greek *drachma;* see *post*, page 38, where allusion is made to *dirhems* having the sign of the cross. The value of the *dirhem* is $6\frac{4}{11}$th *anas*, or about $9\frac{1}{2}$d; (*Galloway on the Law and Constitution of India*, p. iii); but see *post*, p. 77, note 4.

[2] Arab . *Rootbut*,—applied generally to all kinds of green vege-tables, but more particularly such as remain in the ground for several years, (*Inayah*, vol. ii., p. 589,) and have no fixed time of maturity, but may be cut at any time. (*Kifayah*, vol. iv., p. 1007.) Mr. Hamilton describes the land on which five *dirhems* are due as "every *joreeb* of pasture land," (*Hedaya*, vol. ii. p. 207); but *Rootbut* is the term in the original, and grass, the principal growth of pasture land, is common property. See *Moohummudan Law of Sale* (*Baillie*), p. 147, note.

[3] These were the rates imposed by the *Khuleef Omar* on the Sowad of Irak (*Hidayah*, vol. ii., p. 776); and they were adjusted to the different kinds of crops, according to the different degrees of labour required in their cultivation, that on orchards being least, because the trees continue for a long time; on arable lands being greatest, because they require to be cultivated and sown every year; and the labour on *Rootbut* being intermediate, because they are calculated to last for several years. *Inayah*, vol. ii, p. 588.

[4] *Bostan*, a Persian word.

[5] The arabic word *kirm* signifies, among other meanings, a grape-vine, and from the entanglement of the trees might perhaps be more properly translated a vineyard; but it appears that there are other trees, as well as vines, in a *kirm*, and its distinctive character is that the trees (vines, or date), are so closely planted as to prevent the sowing of the intermediate ground. *Hidayah*, vol. ii., p. 776.

Jureeb is the name of an area of sixty by sixty *moolkee ziras;* and a *moolkee zira* is seven hands; being one hand in excess of the common *zira,* (so much is expressed in the book of *Ooshr and Khiraj.*) The Sheikh ool Islam, known as Khwahir Zaduh, has said, that Moohummud, in describing the jureeb as an area of sixty by sixty *ziras,* referred to the *jureeb* then in use, and that it is not a fixed quantity for all lands, but that the *jureeb* of land changes with the change of countries; hence, regard will be had, in every country, to what is well known among its people; and further, that he meant by a *kufeez,* a *saa,* which is eight rutls[1] of Irak, and that is four *minas;* (this was the opinion of Aboo Huneefa and Moohummud, and the first opinion of Aboo Yoosuf); and that this *kufeez* is a *kufeez* of wheat, (so he has stated in one place of the book of *Ooshr* and *Khiraj,* but in another place of it he has stated that it is a *kufeez* of whatever grain is sown in that land, which is correct). And it should further be said, that it is a *kufeez,* with the addition of two handfulls; which some explain by saying that he meant that the measurer should put up his hands on both sides of the *kufeez* at the time of measuring from the heap, and holding fast all that is taken up of the grain between his hands, should place the whole of what is in the *kufeez,* and in his two hands, into the sack of the collector;[2] while others say, that he meant that the measurer should fill the *kufeez,* then draw his hand over the top so as to level all above it, and empty the *kufeez* into the sack of the collector,

[1] The *rutl,* in Egypt, according to Mr. Lane, is 144 *dirhems* in weight, and varies from 15 oz. 10 dr. $22\frac{1}{16}$ gr., to nearly 15 oz. 13 dr., avoirdupois (*Modern Egyptians,* vol ii., p. 371), or a little less than 1 lb. The *rutl* of Irak is somewhat less; if, as seems probable, it be the same as the *rutl* of Bagdad, which is described as containing 20 *astars* of $4\frac{1}{2}$ *mithkals* each (*Fut. Alum.* vol. i., p. 269); that is, taking the *mithkal,* according to Mr. Lane, at $1\frac{1}{2}$ *dirhems,* the *rutl* of Irak would be only 135 *dirhems.* That the *rutl* or *saa* was not a very large quantity, is evident from half a *saa* of wheat or barley being what a good Mooslim is required to give the poor as alms at the *Fitr,* for each member of his family.

[2] Arab. *Ashir,* literally tithesman.

after which he is to fill his two hands from the heap and empty them also into the sack, in addition to the *kufeez.*[1]

The above quantity is due only once a year, whether the proprietor sow his lands once or more than once; contrary to the case of the *Mookasimah Khiraj*, and the *Ooshr*, for there what is due being a part of the actual produce, it is to be repeated as often as the produce is renewed.[2]

To be occasionally reduced when the crops are deficient.

What we have reported as to the quantity of the *Khiraj*, has reference to a case where lands are able to bear so much, but when they are not able to bear so much by reason of a falling off of the crop, the quantity is to be reduced to what the land can bear. A reduction then from the *Wuzeefa* of Omar where the land is unable to bear that *Wuzeefa*, is lawful, according to all opinions.[3] But is an addition to this *Wuzeefa* lawful, when the land is able to bear it, by reason of an abundant crop? On lands where the *Wuzeefa* actually issued from Omar himself, it is not lawful, according to all opinions; and in like manner, on lands where the *Wuzeefa* was imposed by an Imam, in express accordance with the example of Omar, the addition is also unlawful, according to all opinions, even though the addition can be borne.[4] So also, if it should happen, that the same Imam who imposed the *Wuzeefa*, after the example of Omar, should wish to make an addition to that *Wuzeefa*, it would not be competent to him to do so, though the lands were able to bear it. And in like manner, if he should wish to convert that *Wuzeefa* into one of a different kind, as, for instance, if the first *Wuzeefa* were *dirhems*, and he should wish to convert it to the *Mookasimah*, or if it were *Mookasi-*

Can it be lawfully increased when they are abundant.

[1] The authority for the last paragraph is not given by the compilers of the *Futawa Alumgeeree.*

[2] No authority cited.

[3] This is confirmed by the *Hidayah*, vol. ii. p. 777, *Translation* vol. ii. p. 208; and see *post*, p. 64; from which it would seem that the Sooltan cannot lawfully exact the full *Wuzeefa* in such a case, but must take the *Khiraj Mookasimah.*

[4] It is stated in the *Hidayah*, without any qualification, that the addition is lawful, according to Moohummud, and unlawful according to Aboo Yoosuf. (*Translation*, vol. i. p. 208.) The significant words "*and this is approved*" are added, but they do not appear in the printed copy of the original.

mah, and he should wish to convert it to *dirhems*, that would not be in his power. If then he should make an addition upon them, (that is the people,) to this *Wuzeefa*, or convert it from one kind to another, and pass an order upon them to that effect, such being according to his judgment, and he should be succeeded by another ruler who entertains an opposite opinion on the subject, then, if the first ruler acted with their consent, the second ruler may pass, or give currency to what the first did; and though the first had acted without their consent, yet if the lands had been forcibly subdued, and then bestowed upon them by the Imam, the second ruler might also give effect to what the first did. But if the lands were subdued peaceably, before the Imam prevailed against them, and the other circumstances of the case remain the same, the second ruler will cancel the act of the first.[1]

It may be increased with their consent.

And apparently without their consent in one case.

With regard to lands on which the Imam is about to impose a *Wuzeefa* for the first time, if he should exceed the *Wuzeefa* of Omar, it would be lawful according to Moohummud, and one of two reports of Aboo Yoosuf's opinion, but according to Aboo Huneefa, and another report of Aboo Yoosuf it would not be lawful; and this is correct.[2] With regard to the *Mookasimah Khiraj*, it is committed to the Imam to fix the amount, but not so as to exceed the half of the crop.[3]

No higher rates than the *Wuzeefa* of Omar can be lawfully imposed upon land, except the rate is *Mookasimah*.

Khiraj is to be taken from every one who has become the proprietor of *Khirajee* land, whether infidel or mooslim, minor or adult, or whether free, *mookatib*,[4] or *mazoon* slave,[5] or whether man or woman.[6] (*Moheet.*)

Every proprietor of *Khiraj* land must pay the *Khiraj*.

[1] No authority is cited by the compilers of the *Futawa Alumgeeree*, and it is evident that the above has reference only to the *Wuzeefa* of one year, when the crop is more than usually abundant.

[2] It seems to follow *a fortiori* that a *Wuzeefa* once established, cannot be permanently altered to the detriment of the people.

[3] The authority is not cited.

[4] A slave with whom his master has entered into a contract of emancipation for a ransom.

[5] One licensed by his master to trade.

[6] As it is the proprietor of the land who is liable for *Khiraj*, it seems superfluous to remark that the Sooltan or

Wukf land is subject to *Ooshr* and *Khiraj*.

Ooshr and *Khiraj* are due on *wukf* lands.[1] (*Wujeez-ool-Kurdery.*)

Usurpation of *Khiraj* land—how it affects the owner's liability.

Land, the *Khiraj* of which is *Wuzeefa*, has been usurped by an usurper. If the usurper should deny the fact, and the proprietor[2] be without proof; then, supposing that the usurper has not sown the land, no one is liable for the *Khiraj*; but if he have sown the land, and the sowing has not endamaged it, the *Khiraj* is on the usurper. If, on the other hand, the usurper had acknowledged the usurpation, or the proprietor had proof of the fact, and the land were not endamaged by the sowing, the landlord[3] would be liable, and if it were endamaged by the sowing, he would also be liable, according to Aboo Huneefa, whether the damage were little or much, in the same way as if he had let the land to the usurper with responsibility for damage.[4] And in a *Bye-al-wufa*,[5] when the purchaser has taken possession, he is in the same position as an usurper. If one should let his *Khirajee* land, or lend it, he would be liable for the *Khiraj*, in the same way as if he had given it up in *moozaraut*,[6] except

Liability in the case of mortgage.

Lease, or loan.

ruler cannot be the proprietor. But to put this point beyond the possibility of doubt, it is expressly stated in the *Hidayah* "that the lands of the Sowad (on which Omar first imposed the *Khiraj*) are the property of the inhabitants, who may lawfully sell or otherwise dispose of them." Vol. ii. p. 775; *Translation*, vol. ii. p. 205.

[1] Lands settled to pious or charitable uses.

[2] Arab. *Malik*.

[3] Arab. *Rub-ool-Urz*, literally lord or master of the land. The same person who is called *malik*.

[4] The passage is obscure, but its meaning seems to be, that where there is proof of the usurpation, the proprietor is liable for the *Khiraj*, whether the land be damaged by the sowing or not; and that when there is no such pooof, the usurper is liable when the land is not damaged; but it seems left open to doubt who is liable for the *Khiraj* in this case, when the land *is* damaged; see *post*, page 30. Without an express agreement, a hireling or lessee is not responsible for damage, according to Aboo Huneefa. *Hamilton's Hedaya*, vol. iii., p. 350.

[5] Conditional sale or mortgage.

[6] A co-partnership in cultivation between a proprietor of land and a cultivator.

when it is an orchard, or under vegetables or trees closely planted or entangled together.[1] (*Futawa Kazee Khan.*)

Liability as to *Ooshree* land when let to hire.

If *Ooshree* land be let to hire, the *Ooshr* is on the landlord, according to Aboo Huneefa, but on the tenant, according to both his companions. If *Ooshree* land be lent, and sown by the borrower, there are two reports of Aboo Huneefa's opinion. If land fit for sowing be let to hire, or lent, and the hirer or borrower should plant it with vines, or make it into a vegetable ground, the *Khiraj* would be on the hirer or borrower, according to Aboo Huneefa and Moohummud.[2] If *Ooshree* land be usurped and sown, and no damage done by the sowing, the landlord is not liable for *Ooshr*, but if damage be done by the sowing, he is liable for *Ooshr*, in the same way as if he had let the land with the damage.[3] (*Futawa Kazee Khan.*)

When usurped.

Sale of *Khirajee* land, adjustment of liability between seller and purchaser.

A man having *Khirajee* land, sells it at a time that it is quite void; if so much of the year remain as to allow of the purchaser's sowing the land, he is liable for the *Khiraj*, whether he sow it or not; but if enough of the year does not remain to admit of this, the seller is liable for the *Khiraj*, and they say that whether the seed be wheat, or barley, or whatever it may be, the period should be such as to allow the crop to ripen, or to attain to such a degree of forwardness as to be worth double the *Khiraj*. On this point there are various opinions, but, according to the *futwah*, the prescribed time is three months; and if so much should remain, the purchaser would be liable; if not, the liability would fall on the seller. (*Futawa Koobra.*) But suppose that a person should purchase *Khirajee* land, and that before it has been in his possession a sufficient time to enable him to sow it, the Sooltan should take the *khiraj* from him; it would not be competent to the purchaser to have recourse against the seller. (*Futawa Kazee Khan.*) But when the

[1] It seems to be implied in the excepted cases, from the nature of the land, that the lease is for several years.

[2] It seems also implied here that the lease is for several years.

[3] The meaning seems to require "with responsibility for the" damage. See *ante*, p. 8, note 4.

Sooltan takes it from a cultivator, the land being in his possession, and he is unable to prevent it, he has a right of recourse against the proprietor. According to the *Zahir Rewayut*, however, he has no recourse, and this is correct.[1] (*Wujeez-ool-Kurdery.*) If the land yield two crops, the autumnal and spring, and one is delivered to the seller, and one to the purchaser, or each of them has it in his power to reap one of the crops, they are both liable for the *Khiraj*. (*Moheet.*) A man sells *Khirajee* land, and the purchaser sells it to another, after a month; the second then sells it to a third, in like manner, so that the year expires, and the land has not been the property of any of them for three months;—none of them is liable for the *Khiraj*. They say, however, that the correct view of this case is to look to the last purchaser, and if the property remained in his hands for three months, he would be liable for the *Khiraj*.[2] A person sells land in which there is a crop not yet arrived at maturity, and he sells it with the crop; the purchaser is liable for the *Khiraj* under all circumstances. And if he sell it after the grain has fixed or set, and the crop has attained to maturity, the lawyer Aboo Leeth has said, that the case is the same as if he were to sell land void of any crop, and sell with it some reaped wheat. This that we have stated has reference to a time when the *Khiraj* was usually taken at the end of the year, but if it be taken in the beginning of the year by way of advance, that is mere oppression, and neither seller nor purchaser liable. A man has a village in his *Khirajee* land, in which there are houses and lodgings; nothing is due on account of the village, whether he receive grain from it or not.[3] And in

Khiraj is not due on the rent of houses in *Khirajee* land,

[1] This must, I think, be understood only of the case where the land has not been in the cultivator's possession for three months, and the Sooltan's act is therefore oppressive and unlawful,-for otherwise the owner would be liable, as already stated, whether the land had been put into the cultivator's possession under a *moozaraut*, or a lease.

[2] This is, I think, the meaning, but it would seem that the possession must be carried on into the following year.

[3] The grain being a rent for the houses, not for the land. Here, it may be remarked, that the land and the village are both

like manner, when a man has a mansion bounded or marked out in a Mooslim city, and makes it into a garden, or plants it with palm trees and separates it from his lodging, there is nothing due for it, because what remains of the land follows the mansion.[1] But if he make the whole of the mansion into a garden, *Ooshr* is due for it if in *Ooshree* land, and *Khiraj* if in *Khirajee* land. A man buys *Khirajee* land and builds a mansion upon it; he is liable for *Khiraj*, though there should be nothing left capable of tillage.

nor on the ground of a mansion, when sown or planted.

When the Sooltan has given the *Khiraj* to the owner[2] of the land and left it on him,[3] it is lawful, according to a saying of Aboo Yoosuf, which however is contrary to one of Moohummud; but the *futwa* is in accordance with the saying of Aboo Yoosuf; when the owner of the land is one of the class entitled to *Khiraj*,[4] and on this principle it would be lawful in favour of Kazees and lawyers.[5] When the Sooltan has not made any demand for *Khiraj* of the person by

Application of the *Khiraj* by the *Sooltan* to the owner of the land —when lawful.

said to belong to a person to whom the villagers pay rent in corn for their dwellings. It is obvious that *they* are not the proprietors.

[1] Nothing is due for a mansion. *post*, p. 28, note 1.

[2] Arab. *Sahib-ool-Urz*, literally, companion of the land. "This word (Sahib) is much used in composition, to denote the master or possessor of any quality or thing," as "*Sahib-i-tukht*, possessor of a throne, a king;" "*Sahib-ool-mal*, a wealthy proprietor." *Richardson's Persian and Arabic Dictionary*. I prefer "*owner* or *proprietor* to *possessor*," because in the contract of *Moozaraut* the possession of the land must be with the cultivator, while the proprietor is termed *Sahib*.

[3] That is, without demanding payment.

[4] Literally, the people of *Khiraj*.

[5] The following are the objects and persons on whom the *Khiraj* is to be expended, viz.: Donations to the troops, securing the passes, erecting fortifications, establishing watch-houses in the Mooslim territory as a protection against highway thieves, repairing bridges, clearing the channels of great rivers that have no proprietors, such as the Oxus, the Tigris, and Euphrates, building of caravanseras and places of worship, repairing breaches in embankments, providing for governors and their assistants, and *Kazees*, *Moofties*, and police, and the teachers and students of learning, and every person employed in serving the Mooslims, or otherwise generally for the benefit of believers. *Futawa Alum.* vol. i. p. 268.

whom it is due, it is incumbent on the owner of the land to expend it in charity; but if he should expend it in charity after a demand has been made, he would not be released from his obligation.[1] When an Amil has left the *Khiraj* on a *Moozarea*,[2] without the knowledge of the Sooltan, it is lawful, though a disbursement.[3]

Application of *Ooshr* by the Sooltan to the owner of the land—is not lawful.

Moohummud has said, that when the Sooltan has given the *Ooshr* to the owner of the land, it is not lawful, and about this there is no difference of opinion.[4] But the Sheikh-ool-Islam has related, that when the Sooltan has left the *Ooshr* on the owner of the land, the case is to be considered in two ways; first, when he has left it through neglect, by reason of forgetfulness, and here it is incumbent on the person who is liable for the *Ooshr* to expend its amount on the poor; and second, when the Sooltan has left it intentionally with his knowledge, and this case also presents two aspects; if the person who is liable for the *Ooshr* be rich, the Sooltan's act is lawful, but he must make good the amount from the *Khiraj* treasury to the *Alms* treasury;[5] and if the

[1] It is obvious that what is above stated of the application of *Khiraj*, has reference only to the *Khiraj* of the year or particular time, not to the right to it in future.

[2] The cultivator under a contract of *Moozaraut*.

[3] The expression is obscure. It probably means, that though it is the duty of the *Amil* to collect the revenue, not to disburse it, and this is tantamount to a disbursement, still it is lawful. The case may refer to land where the cultivator is the *Moozarea* of the Sooltan, that is, where there is no intermediate proprietor between them, for it is said, that the *Khiraj* is *on* the *Moozarea*, or that he is liable for it. In the contract of *Moozaraut*, the words *Amil* and *Moozarea* are usually applied to the same person, that is, the cultivator, which makes some further obscurity in the passage. I have adopted the construction in the text, taking the word *Amil* to signify "a collector of the revenue" (*Richardson*;) a sense in which it is still used by native governments in India, and is sometimes employed in the *Futawa Alumgeeree*, See vol. i. p. 264.

[4] That is, that such was his opinion.

[5] There are four departments of the *Beit-ool-mal*, or public treasury. The first is for the *Zukat* of flocks and herds, *ooshr* or tithes, and what is taken by the tithesman from Mooslim merchants who go to him; the second, for the *fifths* of plunder, mines, and buried treasures; the third, for the *Khiraj*, the *Jizyut*, and

person on whom the *Ooshr* is, be poor and in need of it, the leaving of it upon him is lawful, and the *Ooshr* is as alms to him, and lawful in the same way as if it had been first taken from, and then expended upon him. (*Zukheerah.*)

Khiraj is due though land be untilled,

Moohummud has said, in the *Jama Sugheer*, that a man having *Khirajee* land, who allows it to remain idle, is liable for the *Khiraj*. (*Moheet.*) But this is when the Khiraj is *Moowuzzuf;* for when the *Khiraj* is *Mookasimah* nothing is due under such circumstances. (*Siraj-ool-Wuhhaj.*) They say, that when a man changes to the lower of two kinds of cultivation without excuse, he is liable for the *Khiraj* of the higher; as for instance, if one who had saffron lands, should sow them with grain, and abandon the cultivation of saffron, he would be liable for the *Khiraj* of saffron; and in like manner, if he had an orchard, and were to cut it down, and sow the land with grain, he would be liable for the *Khiraj* of orchards. This is obvious or proper, but decisions are not given to that effect, lest they should lead to the oppression of men's property.[1] (*Kafee.*)

or the owner is converted to the Mooslim faith.

Where a person who is subject to *Khiraj* has embraced the faith of Islam, *Khiraj* is to be taken from him as before; and it is lawful for a Mooslim to purchase *Khirajee* land from a *Zimmee*, but *Khiraj* will be taken from him. (*Hidayah.*)

Ooshr and *Khiraj* cannot both be taken for the same land.

Ooshr and *Khiraj* are not joined together in the same land, whether the land be *Ooshree* or *Khirajee;* and if one should purchase *Ooshree* or *Khirajee* land to trade with, he would be liable for *Ooshr* or *Khiraj*, as the case might be, without the *Zukat* for trade. (*Moheet.*) When a *Zimmee* has purchased *Ooshree* land, Aboo Huneefa and Zoofr have said that *Khiraj* should be taken from him.[2] (*Zad.*)

what the Beni Nujran and Beni Tooghlib have compounded for, and also what is collected by the tithesman from Moostamins, (foreigners under protection,) and *Zimmee* merchants; and the fourth for troves. *Futawa Alumgeeree*, vol. i. p. 268.

[1] The meaning is, that though strictly in accordance with principle, and lawful to exact the higher rate in the cases supposed, yet that the power is so liable to abuse, that it is not to be countenanced by the judge's decree. *Inayah*, vol. ii., p. 590.

[2] According to Aboo Yoosuf he will be liable to a double

Course to be pursued by ruler when persons subject to *Khiraj* are unable to cultivate their land.

If a family[1] or set of persons subject to *Khiraj*, is unable to prepare their lands or reap the produce, and pay their *Khiraj*, the Imam is not at liberty to take their lands from them, and deliver them to other parties by way of a transfer of the property. (*Zukheerah.*) Mohummud has said, in the book of *Ooshr* and *Khiraj*, that if the owner of *Kirajee* land be unable to cultivate it, and allows it to lie idle, or abandons it, the Imam is at liberty to deliver it to any one who will abide upon it, and pay the *Khiraj*. Hulwaee, however, has said, (and it is the sound answer to give in this case,) that the Imam should first let the lands to hire, take the rent, and deduct the *Khiraj* from it, and keep the remainder for the landlord, (and Moohummud has reported to the same effect in the *Zeeaduh*); but if he cannot find a person who will take the land on hire, he should then deliver it in *Moozaraut* for a third or fourth of the produce, according to the rate at which such land is usually taken at in *Moozaraut*, and deduct the *Khiraj* from the share of the owner, and hold the remainder for the landlord;[2] and if he cannot find a person who will take the land in *Moozaraut*, he will deliver it to any one who will abide upon it and pay its *Khiraj*. (The manner in which this is held to be legal is in one of two ways; it is either placing the parties to whom the land is delivered in the situation of the proprietor, (*malik*) as to the cultivation of the land and payment of the *Khiraj*, or it is leasing the land for the amount of the *Khiraj*, the sum taken from the parties being *Khiraj* as regards the Imam, and hire or rent with regard to themselves.) He has further said, that if the Imam cannot

Ooshr, and according to Moohummud to a single *Ooshr*, to be applied to the purposes of *Khiraj*. *Hamilton's Hedaya*, vol. i. p. 50.

[1] Arab. *Kowm*. A little further on it is applied to so few as two persons, who do not appear to be connected together further than by their combining in a purchase.

[2] It will be observed that the words owner (*sahib*) and lord (*rub*) are here indifferently applied in the same sentence to the person liable for the *Khiraj*, that is, the proprietor of the land.

find a person who will work the land for the *Khiraj*, he may sell it and deduct the *Khiraj* from the price, reserving the remainder for the landlord. It has been said by some, that what has been related of the Imam's selling the land, was only the opinion of Aboo Yoosuf and Moohummud, and that according to Aboo Huneefa, it is not proper that he should sell; for selling ones property is inhibiting himself, and Aboo Huneefa did not approve of the inhibition of free persons; but it has also been said that it was the opinion of them all, and this is correct, for Aboo Huneefa allowed of inhibition in circumstances where it was for the general good.[1] It is reported in some books upon this case, that the Imam should purchase cattle and implements of husbandry, and commit the land to some one to cultivate it, and when the crop is obtained take from it the amount of the *Khiraj*, together with what he has expended upon it, and keep the remainder for the landlord. And Aboo Yoosuf has said, that the Imam should lend the owner of the land from the public treasury as much as will enable him to buy cattle and implements of husbandry, and take from him a deed, binding himself to cultivate the land, and when the grain is ripe he may take from it the *Khiraj*, and what he lends him will be a debt against the owner of the land. He has also said, that if there be nothing in the public treasury, he should deliver the land to one who will abide upon it, and pay the *Khiraj*. When a landlord is unable to cultivate his land, and the Imam has acted in the manner abovementioned, and subsequently the landlord's power and ability to work and cultivate returns, the Imam should demand back the land from the person in whose hands it may happen to

[1] "The causes of inhibition are three: infancy, insanity, and servitude." *Hamilton's Hedaya*, vol. iii., p. 468. In this the three doctors agreed, but they differed as to "weakness of mind," which Aboo Yoosuff and Moohummud thought a sufficient ground, viewed with reference to the individual himself, but Aboo Huneefa thought insufficient, unless when required for the public good, as, for instance, in the case of an ignorant physician, &c. *Ibid.* p. 473.

be, and restore it to its owner, except only in the case of its having been sold. (*Moheet.*)

When they abandon the land altogether.

When people subject to *Khiraj*[1] run away and abandon their lands, Husn has related, as from Aboo Huneefa, that the Imam has an option, and may if he please, cultivate the land from the public treasury, when the produce will belong to the Mooslims, or if he please he may deliver it to others, and settle a rate upon it, of so much for each *jureeb*,[2] and what is taken from them will belong to the public treasury; and he has related as from Aboo Yoosuf, that when people subject to *Khiraj* die,[3] the Imam should deliver their lands in *Moozaraut*, or if he please, let them, and place the hire or rent in the public treasury; and if they run away he should let the land, and take the amount of the *Khiraj* from it, and keep the remainder for the people, and restore it to them when they return; but he should not let the lands until the expiration of the year in which they have run away. (*Siraj-ool-Wuhhaj*).

When it is lawful to transfer *Zimmees* from their own to other lands

The transfer of *Zimmes* from their own to other lands is valid, upon sufficient reason; and it is a sufficient reason that they have no courage nor strength, and are exposed to the attack of enemies, or that there is any fear of their betraying the secrets of Mooslims to the enemy. But they are entitled to the value of their lands, or to the like quantity

[1] Literally "people of *Khiraj*." The Arabic word *uhl* (translated people) is frequently used to signify an individual; but being here preceded by a verb in the singular, and followed by other verbs in the plural, it is, I think, to be taken as a collective noun, and may indicate a *family*, like the word *kowm* in the case on page 14. It also seems that the land, like the estate, a little further on, is subject to one entire *Khiraj*.

[2] This corresponds with the explanation of the original word *mookataut*, which is given in the translation of a firman by the Emperor Aurungzebe, of which a copy will be found in the Appendix. The word means literally "reciprocal cutting," as if the *Khiraj* and the land were cut or divided into parts proportioned to each other.

[3] The word *uhl* is here also preceded by a verb in the singular, and it is evident from the reference to "their lands," and the rest of the sentence, that it is to be taken in a collective sense. The case seems to suppose the total extermination of a family or set of persons subject to *Khiraj*, and the absence of any heirs or claimants of the land.

by measurement of other lands, and will be liable for the *Khiraj* of the land to which they are transferred. There is one report, however, according to which they would be liable for the *Khiraj* of the land from which they had been transferred; but the first is more correct; and their lands are *Khirajee,* so that if afterwards occupied by a Mooslim, he would be liable for *Khiraj.* (*Kafee.*)

Course to be followed by the Sooltan when the proprietors of a village are dead or absent, and the villagers wish to surrender it.

The lords or proprietors of a village in which there are *Khirajee* lands are dead or absent, and the villagers being unable to pay its *Khiraj,* wish to surrender it to the Sooltan; in such circumstances the Sooltan will do as we have said, and if he wish to take the village to himself, he will sell it to another, and buy it from the purchaser.[1] (*Futawa Kazee Khan.*)

Khiraj of an estate to be rateably divided when purchased by several persons jointly.

A family of persons purchase an estate,[2] in which there are orchards and lands; one of them purchasing the orchards, and the other the lands, and they wish to divide the *Khiraj.* It has been said, that if the *Khiraj* of the orchards be known, and the *Khiraj* of the lands be also known, they will remain subject to the same order as before the purchase; but if the *Khiraj* of the orchards be unknown, and the *Khiraj* of the estate has been one entire sum, and it is known that the orchards were orchards originally, and never known but as orchards, and the same is the case as to the lands, regard will be had to the *Khiraj* of orchards and of lands; and if this be ascertained, the whole *Khiraj* of the estate will be divided upon the parties, according to the amount of their shares. (*Futawa Kazee Khan.*)

Claim for equalization of *Khiraj* in a village—how to be adjusted.

There is a village on the lands of which the *Khiraj* is variously assessed, and a person whose land is subject to a greater proportion of the *Khiraj,* demands an equalization as between himself and the others. It is said that if it cannot be ascertained whether the *Khiraj* was originally equal or different, it should be left as before.[3] (*Futawa Kazee Khan.*)

[1] Here also, it must be evident, that the villagers are not the proprietors. Compare with *ante,* page 10, note 3.

[2] Arab. *Zeeut.*

[3] Here it would appear that the villagers are the proprietors,

It is stated in some Futawa, that when a man converts his *Khirajee* land into a tomb, or a corn exchange for merchants, or into dwellings for the poor, the *Khiraj* drops or ceases.[1]

When the *Khiraj* falls into arrear, the whole is to be exacted.

When a Mooslim is allowed to fall into arrears for the *Khiraj* of his land, for two years, the whole of the arrear should be taken from him, according to Aboo Yoosuf and Moohummud, but only the *Khiraj* of the current year, according to Aboo Huneefa. Sheikh ool Islam has reported to this effect in his lesser commentary on the Institutes, but Sudur ool Islam, in a book on the *Ooshr* and *Khiraj*, has given two reports from Aboo Huneefa, and has said that what is correct is, that the whole should be taken. (*Moheet.*)

No *Khiraj* is due from land which cannot be cultivated,

There is no *Khiraj* when water has over-flooded the land, or is cut off from it, or prevents its cultivation. (*Nuhr-ool-Faik.*) Moohummud has related in the *Nawadir,* that when *Khirajee* land has been submerged in water, and the water has subsided in time to allow of a second crop, before the entrance on a second year, and the owner neglects to cultivate it, he is liable for the *Khiraj,* but that if the water has not subsided in time to allow of a second crop before the entrance upon a second year, the *Khiraj* is not due. (*Moheet.*)

or when the crop is distroyed by any providential calamity.

When a providential calamity happens to the crop, which could not be prevented, such as inundation, conflagration, excessive cold, and the like, there is no *Khiraj;* but when the calamity is not providential, and could have been prevented, such as eating by apes, wild beasts, cattle, and the like, the *Khiraj* does not drop; (and this is correct); and Sheikh ool Islam has related that the loss of the crop, before it has been reaped, causes the *Khiraj* to drop, but that its loss after it has been reaped, does not cause the *Khiraj* to drop. (*Siraj-ool-Wuhhaj.*)

When *Ooshr* drops, and the

In *Ooshree* land, when the crop has perished before being reaped, the *Ooshr* drops, and if it have perished after

for they are liable to the *Khiraj,* and there is no one between them and the sovereign. There is, however, nothing like a republic of villagers, for they are evidently liable each for his own land.

[1] The authority is not cited.

being reaped, so much of the *Ooshr* as corresponds to the share of the landlord drops, and so much of it as corresponds to the share of the cultivator[1] remains on the liability of the landlord. And the *Khiraj Mookasimah* is in the same predicament as the *Ooshr*, for what is due in both cases is something out of the actual crop, and the *Ooshr* differs only as to the objects on which it is expended.[2] This is when the whole of the produce has perished; and if the greater part has perished, and some remains, regard will be had to what remains, and if what remains be equal to two *kufeezees* and two *dirhems*, one *kufeez* and one *dirhem* are due, and the *Khiraj* does not drop, and if less than this remains, half the crop is due. (*Futawa Kazee Khan.*) Our elders have said that what is proper in the case, is to look first to what the man has expended on the land, and then to deduct what has been expended from the produce, and if any thing remain, to take from it as we have explained. (*Siraj-ool-Wuhhaj* and *Moheet.*)

destruction of the crop.

The *Khiraj* indeed drops with the loss of the crop, when there does not remain enough of the year for one to cultivate the land; but if so much does remain the *Khiraj* does not drop; and the effect is the same, as if the first occurrence had not taken place. And in like manner, with regard to an orchard, when its fruit is taken away by any calamity, but part only is taken away, while part remains, and the remainder amounts to twenty *dirhems* or more, ten *dirhems* are due; but if what remains do not amount to twenty *dirhems*, half of what remains is due; and so also, in the case of vegetables. (*Futawa Kazee Khan.*)

Praiseworthy conduct of the *Khoosroes.*

It was praiseworthy in the conduct of the Khoosroes[3] that when calamity overtook the crop of the *Moozarea*, they used to indemnify him for his seed and maintenance out of the treasury, and to say, "the *Moozarea* is our partner in profit, how then, shall we not share with him in loss." And a

[1] Arab. *Akkar*, from *Akr* digging. A digger or tiller of the ground.

[2] It would seem that in other respects the *Ooshr* and *mookasimah Khiraj* are subject to the same rules.

[3] The Persian Dynasty that immediately preceded the Mahomedan Conquest.

Mooslim Sooltan in such dispositions is superior to them.[1] (*Wujeez-ool-Kurdery.*)

How arable land is to be assessed when planted with fruit trees.

A man plants a vine in *Khiraj* land; till the vine bear he is liable for the *Khiraj* of arable land; and in like manner if he should plant fruit trees he would be liable for the *Khiraj* of arable land till the trees bear fruit. When the vine arrives at maturity and bears fruit, if the value of the fruit attain to twenty *dirhems* or more, he is liable for ten *dirhems;* if it be less than twenty he is liable to the extent of half the produce; and if half the produce should not amount to a *kufeez* and a *dirhem,* no abatement will be made from the *kufeez* and *dirhem,* because he might have obtained a crop of grain from the land.

No *Khiraj* on a forest, though abounding with game, or trees not bearing fruit.

If there be a forest on one's land abounding with game, he is not liable for *Khiraj.* If there be in his land reeds or tamarisks, or coniferous trees, or willows, or trees not bearing fruit, it will be considered whether he can cut them down, and make it bear grain, and if he fail to do so he will be subject to *Khiraj;* but if the land cannot be made fit for this he is not liable for *Khiraj.*

Other cases in which *Khiraj* is not due, the land being generally unproductive.

And if there be in the midst of *Khirajee* land some land out of which salt rises, whether it be more or less, then in the same way, if he can make it arable, and it is connected with *Khiraj* water, he is liable for *Khiraj;* but if it be not connected with *Khiraj* water, or if there be land in the mountains unconnected with water, *Khiraj* is not due for it. And if there be among *Khirajee* land a piece of ground that is saltish, and does not admit of being cultivated, *Khiraj* is not due for it.[2] (*Futawa Kazee Khan.*)

[1] It would seem from the above that the contract of *Moozaraut,* though perhaps under another name, was familiar to the Persians before the Mahomedan Conquest, and that there was no intermediate proprietor between the sovereign and the *Moozarea,* or cultivator. If the relation between the parties is to be determined by the rules of Mahomedan Law, the sovereign must have been the proprietor of the land, for the contract of *Moozaraut,* as already explained, is a contract of co-partnership between a proprietor of land and a cultivator.

[2] These exemptions follow necessarily, from the principle that the "cause of *Khiraj* is land when actually increasing or capable of increase." See *post,* p. 23.

The time or season of liability to the *Khiraj* is, according to Aboo Huneefa, the beginning of the year, but subject to the condition that the land remains in the hands of the party, productive for a year, either actually or relatively.[1] (*Zukheerah*).

Ruler should appoint a kind superintendent.

It is the duty of the ruler to place over the *Khiraj* a person who will be kind to the people, and just to them in the matter of their *Khiraj*, and to take from them the *Khiraj* gradually, as the crops are produced, so that the whole may be paid up by the end of the crop. By this is meant that the *Khiraj* should be adjusted to the quantity of the crop; so that if the land be sown with the spring and autumnal crops, the superintendent should consider at the time of reaping the spring crop, how much by guess or conjecture the land is likely to bear for the autumnal crop, and if he should be of opinion that the autumnal is likely to be equal to the spring crop, he should make an equal division of the *Khiraj*, and take half the *Khiraj* from the spring crop, and let half remain over for the autumnal crop. And he should do in the same way with pot-herbs; that is he should consider, and if the herbs be of a kind that is cut five times in the year, he will take at each time a fifth of the *Khiraj*, and if they are of a kind that is cut four times he will take at each time a fourth part of the *Khiraj*; and in like manner according to the same analogy in other cases. (*Moheet.*)

When a man dies who is liable for *Khiraj* or *Ooshr*, it will be taken from his estate,[2] and the *Khiraj* will be taken

[1] That is, I suppose, either till the actual completion of the year, or the completion of the season by getting in the crops.

[2] Not generally so far as regards the *Ooshr*, for that can be taken only out of the particular thing (grain or other produce) if in existence, upon which it is due; and the same is apparently true of the *Mookasimah Khiraj*, which seems to be like the *Ooshr* in all respects, except the purposes to which it is applied. The *Wuzeefa Khiraj* is different from both, inasmuch as it is a debt which binds the person, without being restricted to anything in particular out of which it is to be paid. It may, therefore, be deducted from the estate of a deceased person generally, but the others cannot without his special direction by will. Moreover, the person who is liable for the *Wuzeefa Khiraj* may law-

The Sooltan has a lien on the produce for the *Khiraj*.

Khiraj may be lawfully paid in advance.

when the crop has ripened, according to the difference of countries; and it is not lawful for the owner of *Khiraj* lands to eat of their produce till he has paid the *Khiraj*. (*Futawa Kazee Khan.*) Nor should one eat of the grain of *Ooshr* till he has paid the *Ooshr*; and if he should eat of it he is responsible. And the Sooltan has the power of retaining the grain of *Khirajee* land till he has taken the *Khiraj*. (*Zuheereeah.*)

Moohummud has related in the *Nawadir*, that a person may lawfully advance the *Khiraj* of his land for one year or two years; and it is stated in the *Mooutuha*, that when a man has advanced the *Khiraj* of his land, and the land is afterwards submerged in water in the same year, he should receive back what he paid of the *Khiraj*, or that it should be accounted for to him in the *Khiraj* of the next year, if he should cultivate the land. And it is related of Moohummud, with regard to a man who gave the *Khiraj* of his lands for two years, and it was afterwards overflowed, and became part of the Tigris, that he said it ought to be restored to him if still subsisting, but that if already laid out, there is no help for him; meaning thereby that when expended on the soldiers he could not have anything. (*Moheet.*)

fully give bail or security for it, and may be imprisoned in case of non-payment, which is not the case with the other kind of *Khiraj* or the *Ooshr*. *Kifayah*, vol. iii., p. 288.

CHAPTER II.

OF OOSHR AS THE ZUKAT[1] ON FRUITS AND CROPS.

[This Chapter is taken from the *Futawa Alumgeeree*, vol. i. p. 261.]

Description.

THIS is a positive duty,[2] and its cause is land increasing by an actual issue out of it, in opposition to *Khiraj*, the cause of which is land either actually increasing, or capable of increase; for if land be capable, and not sown, *Khiraj* is due for it, but not *Ooshr*. And if any calamity overtake the crop, *Ooshr* is not due. A transfer of property is essential to it; and the condition to be observed in paying it is the same as has been already explained in regard to *Zukat*.[3]

Two conditions of liability to *Ooshr*. First condition.

There are two conditions necessary to render a person liable to *Ooshr*. The first is *Ahleeut*,[4] that is, *Islam*, or being a Mooslim; (this is essential to its commencement, for it does not begin except with a Mooslim, without any difference of

[1] *Zukat* may be generally described as a poor's rate, levied in kind; in law it is defined to be "the giving of property to a poor Mooslim, other than one of the family of Hashim, or his freed man, for the sake of God, and in such a manner as to cut off the giver from any participation in its benefits." *Fut. Alum.* vol. i. p. 239.

[2] Arab. *Furz*. Founded on the saying of the Prophet, "on whatever the earth produces there is *Ooshr*." *Hidayah*, vol. i. p. 569.

[3] Viz. in the first chapter of the Book of *Zukat*. The condition is a present intention at the time of actually paying or setting apart property for the purpose. When a person, at the time of bestowing anything in charity, if asked what he is paying, is in a position to answer, without reflection,—that is a present intention; but if he were to say, "what I have bestowed up to the end of the year I intended to be on account of *Zukat*," that would not be lawful. *Fut. Alum.* vol. i. p. 239.

[4] Literally, worthiness or aptitude.

opinion)[1] and knowledge of its being a duty. But as to understanding and puberty, these are not conditions necessary to liability; for the lands of minors and insane persons are liable to *Ooshr*, since it is a means of preserving[2] the land, and therefore it is that the Imam is empowered to take it forcibly; whereupon the owner of the land ceases to be responsible for it, but in that case he has no reward. And in like manner, if a person who is liable to *Ooshr* should die while the grain is still in existence, the *Ooshr* may be taken out of it, contrary to the case of *Zukat* generally. And thus a right of property in the land is not a condition of liability to *Ooshr*, for it is due on land under *wukf*,[3] or belonging to a *Mazoon*[4] or to a *Mookatib*.[5]

Second condition.

The second condition is that there be a fit and lawful subject, (by which is meant that the land is *Ooshree*, for there is no *Ooshr* on the produce of *Khirajee* land,) and an existing crop, and that the crop be such as is sown with a view or design to some increase of the earth. (*Buhr-oor-Raik.*) Hence there is no *Ooshr* upon wood, grass, reeds, tamarisk trees, or palm branches; for these things bring no increase to the land, but rather deteriorate it. If, however, any profit should be derived from the osiers of willows, or from grass, reeds, or the branches of palm trees, or if there be plane

[1] Aboo Huneefa was of opinion that *Ooshr* can be received only from a Mooslim. The other two did not go so far, but agreed that it can commence only with a Mooslim, though having been once imposed upon land, they thought that it may be subsequently received from a person of a different faith, to whom the land is transferred.

[2] Arab. *Moonut.* The above meaning is put upon the term by the author of the *Kifayah*, who ascribes this virtue to the prayers of the poor (on whom the *Ooshr* is expended) for assistance to the people of Islam against infidels. In like manner *Khiraj* is *moonut*, by reason of its being expended on soldiers, who repel the attacks of enemies. *Kifayah*, vol. i. p. 474.

[3] See *ante*, page 8, note 1.

[4] *Ante*, page 7, note 5.

[5] *Ibid.* note 4. It may be observed that *Islam*, understanding, puberty, and complete property, (which includes right and possession), are all necessary to render a person liable to the *Zukat* generally.

or fir, or pistachio nut trees, on the ground, which are cut down and sold, *Ooshr* would be due on account of them. (*Moheet-oos-Surukhsee.*)

Ooshr is due on the whole produce of the soil.

According to Aboo Hunefa, *Ooshr* is due on every product of the earth, such as wheat, barley, millet, rice, seeds of different kinds, pot herbs, odoriferous herbs, leaves, vegetables, sugar canes, wormwood, water melons, cucumbers, citruls, *bazunjan*,[1] saffron in the flower, and the like, among things that bear fruit,[2] whether it be permanent or not, and whether small in quantity or abundant. (*Futawa Kazee Khan*). And it makes no difference whether the land be watered by rain from the heavens, or by running water, and whether the articles be measured by the *wusk* or not.[3] (*Shurih-Tahavee*). And it is due on flax, and also on its seed, for each of them is a distinct object in the cultivation of the plant. (*Shurih-ool-Mujma*). It is likewise due on nuts and almonds, cummin seed and coriander. (*Moozmirat*). And *Ooshr* is due for honey when found in *Ooshree* land, and in like manner, on manna, when it falls on the green thorn in a person's land (*Khuzanut-ool-Mooftieen*); and on fruit collected from trees which do not belong to any one, as trees in the mountains. (*Zuheereeah*). And there is no *Ooshr* on what is only an accessory to the earth, such as palm and other trees;[4] nor on anything that issues from trees, as

Exceptions.

[1] Produce of the egg plant.

[2] Aboo Huneefa is speaking only of *Ooshree* land; for if a Mooslim be possessed of *Khirajee* land, he must pay the *Khiraj*, (*ante* p. 7,) and *Ooshr* and *Khiraj* are not payable for the same land, (*ante*, p. 13).

[3] The references to quantity and measure allude to differences of opinion between Aboo Huneefa and his two disciples, who, treating *Ooshr* as a branch of *Zukat*, considered that it is due only on fruits of a permanent character, (such, for instance, as, like dates and raisins, admit of being kept when dried,) which are of a nature to be measured by the *wusk*, and when they amount to what is technically called a *nisab*, that is, five *wusks*. The opinion of Aboo Huneefa is founded on the unqualified terms of the saying of the prophet already quoted; the reasons for the opinions of the other two will be found in *Hamilton's Hedaya*, vol. i., p. 45.

[4] Everything which has a stem or trunk, that is not cut down

gum or liquid pitch, because to obtain these is not an object for planting the trees. (*Buhr-oor-Raik.*) Nor is it due on seeds fit only to be sown or used in medicine, such as the seed of the water-melon, the aniseed, and sesame; nor on hemp, or fir trees, nor on the trees of the cotton, bazunjan, frankincense, or fig. (*Khuzanut-ool-Mooftien.*)

If there be a fruit tree within a person's mansion, no *Ooshr* is due for it.[1] (*Shurih-ool-Mujma.*)

Half *Ooshr*

On land watered by the Persian or Arabian wheel, only half *Ooshr* is due. If the land be watered sometimes by running water, and at others by the Arabian wheel, regard is to be had to the larger part of the year; and if the times be equal, half *Ooshr* is due. (*Khuzanut-ool-Mooftien.*)

Time when liability to *Ooshr* commences.

The time for *Ooshr* is that of the springing up of the seed and appearance of the fruit, according to Aboo Huneefa.[2] (*Buhr-oor-Raik.*) If then a person should advance the *Ooshr* of his land before the sowing, it would not be lawful; and if he advance it after the sowing, and after the plant has sprung up, it would be lawful; but if he advance it after the sowing, and before the plant has sprung up, it would, apparently, be unlawful. With regard to fruit, if a person should advance the *Ooshr* after its appearance, it is lawful, but before its appearance it is unlawful, according to the *Zahir Rewayut.*[3] (*Shurih Tahavee.*)

till it becomes a tree, is an accessory to the land, and is therefore included in a sale of it; while deciduous plants, and generally everything which is not permanent, are not included. *Moohummudan Law of Sale*, (*Baillie*) p. 56.

[1] The Arabic word for mansion (*dar*) is defined to be a place comprehended within an enclosure. (*Hamilton's Hedaya*, vol. ii, p. 502); and neither *Ooshr* nor *Khiraj* is due for the land of a mansion, see *post*, page 28, note 1.

[2] An actual transfer of property is essential to *Ooshr*, as already observed,—that is, the obligation cannot be satisfied without a transfer, but this is impossible with regard to things not in existence; accordingly the sale of seed, before it has sprung up, or fruit, before its appearance, is unlawful. *Moohummudan Law of Sale*, (*Baillie*), page 141.

[3] The obligation to *Ooshr* ceases with the loss of the produce, as will be presently seen; and if the *Ooshr* be paid in anticipation, the party advancing it would apparently be entitled to take

Ooshr drops or ceases with the loss of the produce from any other cause than the act of the owner, and when the loss is partial, it ceases in proportion to the loss. When destroyed by any other than the proprietor, he is to take compensation from the destroyer, and pay the *Ooshr;* and if destroyed by himself, he is responsible for the *Ooshr,* which becomes a debt for which he is liable;[1] but it falls by the apostacy and death of the proprietor without a will, after he has destroyed the property.[2] (*Buhr-oor-Raik.*)

Failure of the crop causes a remission of *Ooshr*

A *Toogohlibee*[3] having *Ooshree* land is liable to a double *Ooshr;* and if a *Zimmee* purchase the land from him, it remains in the same condition, according to them,[4] and the effect is the same, according to Aboo Huneefa, when a Mooslim purchases the land from the Tooghlibee, or he himself adopts the faith of Islam; and it makes no difference whether the duplicity be original or subsequently induced. And supposing a Mooslim to be possessed of land which he sells to a *Zimmee* who is not of the Tooghlibee tribe, and the *Zimmee* takes possession of it, he would be liable to *Khiraj*, according to Aboo Huneefa; bnt if the land be taken from him by another Mooslim, under a claim of *Shoofaa* or pre-emption, or if it should be returned to the seller on account of some

Double *Ooshr* is payable by a *Tooghlibee.*

credit for it in his next payment, as is the case with *Zukat* generally. But if the advance be irregularly made, it must be considered as a mere voluntary payment, for which the party making it could take no credit in the event of loss. *Fut. Alum.* vol. i., p. 247.

[1] Otherwise it is not a debt, and therefore cannot be paid out of the general assets of his estate, without a special direction by his will. See *Kifayah*, vol. iii. p. 265, where the author is speaking generally of *Zukat.*

[2] *Islam* is essential to the liability, which therefore ceases upon apostacy; according to the two disciples, an apostate is competent to make a will. *Fut. Alum.* vol. ii. p. 359.

[3] The *Tooghlibees* were a tribe of Christian Arabs, on the confines of the Roman territories, on whom Omar wished to impose the *jizyut* or capitation tax, but on their threatening to join the enemy he entered into a treaty with them, by which it was agreed that they should pay double of what was payable by Mooslims. *Kifayah*, vol. i. p. 501.

[4] The word being in the plural, and not the dual, I suppose it means "them all," viz: the three doctors.

defect in the sale, it would become *Ooshree*, as before. Land in the hands of a minor or woman of the Tooghlibees is the same as if it were in the hands of a man; and nothing is due by a *Mujoosee* on his mansion.[1] (*Hidayah.*)

Effect of conversion by a Mooslim, of his mansion into a garden.

If a Mooslim convert his mansion into a garden, its burden or liability is determined by its water; if watered by *Ooshr* water, it becomes *Ooshree*, and if by *Khiraj* water, it becomes *Khirajee*. This is different from the case of a *Zimmee*, who, when he converts his mansion into a garden, is liable to *Khiraj*, however it may be watered, but his mansion remains free.[2] (*Tubyeen*). The rule is the same with regard to sepulchres. (*Buhr-oor-Raik.*) And if a Mooslim or a Zimmee were to water his land at one time with *Ooshr* water and at another with *Khiraj* water, the former would be liable to *Ooshr*, and the latter to *Khiraj*. (*Miaraj-ood-Duraya*).

Similar conversion by a *Zimmee.*

Ooshr water and *Khiraj* water.

Ooshr water is the water of wells dug and fountains springing up in *Ooshree* land; so also rain from the heavens, and the water of great seas,[3] is *Ooshree*. (*Moheet.*) The water of canals excavated by the Persians,[4] and the water of wells dug in *Khirajee* land is *Khirajee*. And as to the water of the Syhoon, (Jaxartes), the Tigris, and the Euphrates, it is *Khirajee*, according to Aboo Huneefa, and Aboo Yoosuf.[5] (*Kafee.*)

Lease of

If one should let *Ooshree* land to hire, the lessor would be

[1] Because Omar made all dwellings entirely exempt. *Hidayah*, vol. i. p. 537; *Translation*, vol. i. p. 51.

[2] That is the actual dwelling remains exempt.

[3] The Arabic word *Buhar*, which means any large bodies of water, is thus qualified in the *Hidayah*—" which do not enter under the power of any one;" vol. i. p. 537; *Translation*, vol. i. p. 51.

[4] The canals alluded to are probably those by which the waters of the Tigris and Euphrates are distributed over the Sowad of Irak. They were originally excavated, according to the author of the *Lub-ool-Tareekh*, by Manusheher, an ancient king of Persia, of the Peshdadian dynasty, for the convenience of the people, though afterwards converted into a source of public revenue. *D'Herbelot Biblioth. Orient.* and *Sir John Malcolm's History of Persia*, vol. ii. p. 473.

[5] Moohummud thought the waters of these rivers to be *Ooshree*, because no one can prohibit their use. *Hidayah*, vol. ii. p. 537.

liable for the *Ooshr*, according to Aboo Hunefa, but the tenant, according to the other two. (*Khoolasa.*) Should the crop perish before it is reaped, the lessor would not be liable for the *Ooshr*, but if it should perish after being reaped, the *Ooshr* would not drop. According to the other two, however, whether the crop perish before or after being reaped, it would alike perish, with whatever might be on it. (*Shurih Tahavee*). If one should lend his land to a Mooslim, the borrower would be liable for the *Ooshr*, but if he lend it to an infidel, the lender would be liable, according to Aboo Huneefa. According to the other two, however, the infidel would be liable, with this difference between them, that the liability would, in the opinion of Moohummud, be limited to a single *Ooshr*, while in that of Aboo Yoosuf it would extend to two *Ooshrs*. (*Moheet-oos-Surukhsee.*) In a case of *Moozaraut*,[1] the burden would fall upon both parties, in proportion to their shares, according to the two, but in the opinion of Aboo Huneefa, the owner of the land would alone be liable; the liability for his own share being specific, but for that of the *Moozarea* or husbandman, indeterminate. (*Buhr-oor-Raik.*) And if the crop should perish, the *Ooshr* would drop in regard to both parties, according to the two; and so also, in the opinion of Aboo Huneefa, when the loss occurs before the crop is reaped; but if it should not occur till after the reaping, he was of opinion that the owner's liability in regard to the share of the *Moozarea* would not drop, while it would drop in regard to his own share. And supposing that another person should destroy the crop before it is reaped, but after considerable labour had been expended upon it, or should steal it, there would be no *Ooshr* till the destroyer make compensation, whereupon the owner would become liable for a tenth part of the consideration; but according to the other two, both parties would be liable. (*Moheet-oos-Surukhsee.*) And if *Ooshree* land be usurped and sown by the usurper, the owner would not be liable for the *Ooshr*, unless the land were damaged by the sowing, but if it were

Ooshree land.

Loan of such land.

Moozaraut

[1] See *ante*, page 8, note 6.

damaged by the sowing, the burden of the *Ooshr* would be on the owner of the land.[1] (*Khoolasa.*)

Sale of *Ooshree* land.

When *Ooshree* land, in which there is seed that has already ripened, is sold with the seed, or the crop is sold by itself, the seller, and not the purchaser, is liable for the *Ooshr;* and if the crop be pot-herbs, and it is sold, and the herbs are immediately cut by the purchaser, the seller is liable, but if they are left till ripe the *Ooshr* is on the purchaser. (*Shurih Tahavee.*)

Sale of grain subject to *Ooshr.*

When a person has sold grain which is subject to *Ooshr,* the *Moosuddik,* or alms-collector, may take his *Ooshr* from the purchaser, though the parties should have separated;[2] or if he please he may take it from the seller. And suppose that the person had sold the grain for more than its value, and the purchaser had not yet taken possession, the *Moosuddik* might then take either a tenth of the grain or a tenth of the price, at his pleasure; but if the seller had given it at a price much below what men would generally take for it in the circumstances, the *Moosuddik* would have no alternative but to take a tenth of the grain;[3] and if the seller should destroy the grain, the *Moosuddik* may take from him a tenth of similar grain, unless he prefer to give the amount of its value out of the price. And if the purchaser should destroy it, the *Moosuddik* has the option of making either the seller or the purchaser responsible for a tenth of similar grain; for both of them have been instrumental in destroying what was his right. If grapes be sold, the *Ooshr* is to be taken from the price; and in like manner, if they were converted

[1] It may be observed on this and the parallel passage on page 8, that a usurper is not responsible for the *use* of the thing usurped (*Hedaya,* vol. iii. p. 550); consequently he is not liable for rent. But if usurped land be damaged by the cultivation of it, the usurper must compensate for the damage. (*Ibid.* page 527.) In this case, then, he has something against which the *Ooshr* or *Khiraj* may be set; which seems to be the ground of the distinction.

[2] That is, though the sale be completed, which it would be by separation of the parties.

[3] That is, being a public officer, it would be a breach of trust if he took anything much less than the value.

into juice, and then sold, the seller would be liable for a tenth of the price of the juice. (*Moheet-oos-Surukshee.*)

No allowance is made for expenses of cultivation, &c.

The hire of labourers, the keep of cattle, the expense of digging channels, or the hire of a keeper, &c., are not to be taken into account; and the proper rate, whether a tenth or a half, is to be deducted from the gross produce of the earth. (*Buhr-oor-Raik.*)

Ooshr must first be deducted before consumption of any part of grain subject to it.

No part of grain subject to *Ooshr* is to be consumed until the *Ooshr* is paid. (*Zuheereeah.*) But if the *Ooshr* be separated, it is lawful to consume the remainder; and Aboo Huneefa has said that if another person should eat any part of the fruit or grain, the owner is answerable for the *Ooshr*. (*Moheet-oos-Surukhsee.*)[1]

[1] This branch of the *Zukat*, together with that on flocks and herds, &c., (*ante*, p. 12, note 5,) is applicable generally to the following persons and objects. 1st, *Fakeers*, or persons who have property not exceeding a *nisab* in quantity, after the supply of their own wants; 2nd, *Miskeens*, or persons entirely destitute; 3rd, *Amils*, or officers appointed to collect alms and tithes; provided they do not belong to the family of Hashim; 4th, *Rikab*, or assistance to *Mookatibs*, to complete their ransoms; 5th, Debtors who do not possess property above a *nisab*, clear of their debts; 6th, *Subeel oollah*, or the service of God, as enabling poor persons to perform the duties of *jihad* and *hujj*, or religious warfare and pilgrimage; and 7th, Travellers who are cut off from their means of support. *Fut. Alum.* vol. i. p. 263.

CHAPTER III.

OF THE IMPOSITION OF TITHE AND TRIBUTE UPON LAND.

[This Chapter is composed of extracts from different parts of the Book of *Siyur*, *Futawa Alumgeeree*, vol. ii.]

Definition.

Siyur[1] is *jihad*,[2] that is, a call to the true Religion, and war with those who refuse or hesitate to submit to it, either in their persons or their property. Two things are required to justify it; one of these is the refusal of the enemy to accept the true religion when called upon, and the absence of any special protection granted to them, or subsisting treaty between them and us; and the other is a reasonable hope that the people of *Islam* will be endowed with courage and strength to contend with them and their allies. When there is no ground for expecting this, war is unlawful, as being a manifest throwing away of life. The effect or consequence to the individual, is the discharge of a duty incumbent upon him in this world, and obtaining the reward of felicity in the world to come, as in all other acts of devotion. (*Mooheet-oos-Surukhsee.*)[3]

When permitted.

Course to be followed on entering an enemy's country.

When the Imam has determined on entering into the enemy's country, it is incumbent on him to number his armies, horse, and foot, and write down their names. (*Shurih Tahavee.*) And when the Mooslims have entered the enemy's country, and have surrounded a city or fortress, they are to call the inhabitants to *Islam;* if they comply with the call,

Call to *Islam*.

[1] Plural of *Seerut*, custom or institution, but applied in law to the particular institutes or rules by which Mooslims are guided in their intercourse with people of a different religion.

[2] Literally, waging war.

[3] *Fut. Alum.* vol. ii. p. 266.

the Mooslims are to desist from fighting with them; if they refuse, they are to be called upon to pay the *Jizyut* or capitation tax.[1] (*Hidayah.*) And if they accept they are entitled to what we are entitled to, and are subject to what we are subject to. (*Kunz.*) This is to be understood of persons from whom the *Jizyut* may be lawfully accepted; for those from whom it is not lawful to accept the *Jizyut*, are not to be called upon to pay it. (*Tibyeen.*) Infidels are of different kinds. There is one kind from whom it is unlawful to accept the *Jizyut* and to whom the condition of *Zimmut* cannot be conceded. These are the associators[2] of Arabia, who have no sacred writings, and when we conquer them there is no alternative for their men, but the sword or *Islam*, and their women and children are *Fee.*[3] There is another kind from whom it is lawful to accept the *Jizyut* according to general agreement; and these, among people who have sacred writings, are Jews and Christians, whether Arab or of any other nation; and from *Majoosees*, also, it is lawful according to all opinions to take the *Jizyut*, whether they be Arabs or not. There is a third kind with regard to whom there is a difference of opinion as to the lawfulness of accepting *Jizyut* from them; and these are associators not of Arabia, who have neither any sacred writings nor are *Majoosees;* but according to us it is lawful to accept the *Jizyut* from them. (*Moheet.*)

Different kinds of infidels.

It is not lawful to fight with those who have not received the invitation to *Islam*, without calling upon them. (*Hidayah.*)

[1] It is of two kinds. When imposed on a people under capitulation, and with mutual consent, its amount is whatever may be agreed upon, and it cannot be afterwards increased. When imposed on a conquered people it is fixed by law at forty-eight *dirhems* per annum for the rich, twenty-four *dirhems* for persons of middling condition, and twelve *dirhems* for the poor, payable in each case monthly, in equal portions. *Fut. Alum.* vol. ii. p. 347.

[2] Persons who associate any one other object of worship with the Supreme Deity. The term, unless qualified, would include Christians, as well as idolaters.

[3] What is taken from infidels by force and violence in actual warfare, is called *Ghuneemut*, or plunder; what is taken from them when there is no actual war is *Fee*, and it includes *Jizyut* and *Khiraj*. *Fut. Alum.* vol. ii. p. 390.

If they refuse *Islam* and the *Jizyut*, the assistance of God is to be called for against them, and they are to be warred with to the last extremity. (*Ihtiyar-Shurih-ool-Mookhtar*).[1]

How to be treated when they voluntarily submit.

Moohummud has said that when the inhabitants of a city belonging to the enemy embrace the faith before the Mooslims have prevailed against them, they are entirely free, and no legal means remain of assailing them, their children, their women, or property, and the *Ooshr*, not the *Khiraj*, is to be imposed upon their lands. In like manner, if the inhabitants of the city become *Zimmees* or subjects, by submitting to the *Jizyut* without embracing the faith, before they are conquered by the Mahomedans, they are equally free as to their persons, their families, and properties, with this exception, that here the *Khiraj* and not the *Ooshr* is to be imposed on their lands, and the *Jizyut* to be laid on their heads.

When they are conquered.

But if the Mussulmans prevail against them, and they then embrace the faith, the Imam has an option with regard to them, and may if he please divide them, and their property among the soldiers.[2] If such be his intention after the inhabitants have declared their profession of the faith, he ought to deduct a fifth for the benefit of orphans, the poor, and travellers, and make division of the remaining four-fifths among the soldiers, and impose the *Ooshr* upon the lands. But he may, if he please, bestow his grace upon the inhabitants who embrace the faith, and deliver up to them their persons, their families, and property, and impose the *Ooshr*, or fix a *Khiraj* upon their lands, as he may deem proper. When the inhabitants, after being conquered, refuse to embrace the faith, the Imam is at liberty to reduce them to slavery, and divide them and their property among the soldiers. If he intend to adopt this course, he is first to take a fifth from the whole for the purposes above-mentioned, and

[1] The authorities in the two last paragraphs are taken from *Fut. Alum.*, vol. ii. p. 273-4.

[2] The authority for this is derived from the conduct of the Prophet with regard to *Kheiber*; but his example is not considered to form an imperative rule for all occasions, "or why was it departed from by the Khufeef Omar in the case of Irak, with the general consent of the companions?" *Kifayah*, vol. ii. p. 723.

then to divide the remainder among the soldiers, and to impose the *Ooshr* upon the land; or he may if he please slay the adult males, and divide the women, the children, and property among the soldiers. But he may also, if he please, grant the inhabitants their lives and freedom, together with their property, and impose the *Jizyut* on their necks and the *Khiraj* on their lands[1] (*Moheet.*) And in this there is no difference, whether the water be *Ooshree,* like water of the heavens, fountains and wells, or *Khirajee,* as water of the canals dug by the Persians. (*Ghayut-ool-Buyan*). And when the Imam has conquered a country belonging to the enemy, and has divided it and its inhabitants among the soldiers, he cannot afterwards, if so inclined, grant the people their persons and lands; nor when he has once bestowed these upon them, can he afterwards if so inclined, make a division of them. (*Moheet.*)[2]

[1] As was done by Omar with regard to the *Sowad* of Irak, with the concurrence of the companions. It is related of Omar on this occasion, that he consulted the companions as to the lands, and that some said, "They are plunder, divide them among the soldiers," while others were of a different opinion; whereupon Omar postponed the matter, and turned to the *Kooran.* When the morrow came, he said, "I have found in the Book of God what will suffice without your opinions." He then quoted the verse, "and those that come after them, &c.," saying "if I were to divide the land among you, what would there be for those who come after you." Whereupon they all agreed to what he said, with the exception of a small number, including Belal, so insignificant that their opposition is disregarded, and Omar's decision is, therefore, said to have been with the concurrence of the companions. *Hidayah* and *Kifayah*, vol. ii. p. 723.

[2] The authorities in the last paragraph are taken from the *Fut. Alum.* vol. ii. p. 292.

CHAPTER IV.

OF THE KHOOMS,[1] OR FIFTH ON MINES AND BURIED TREASURE.

[This Chapter is taken from the *Futawa Alumgeeree*, vol. i. p. 259.]

Three kinds of products from mines

Metals.

The products of mines[2] are of three kinds. They are either fusible[3] in the fire, or fluid in their own nature,[4] or neither fusible nor fluid. The fusible are such as gold, silver, iron, tin or lead, brass and copper; and upon these a fifth is due,[5] (*Tuhzeeb;*) whether they are extracted by a free person, or a slave, a *Zimmee*, a youth, or a woman; and what remains belongs to the taker.[6] When an alien *Moos-tamin* works without permission of the Imam, he is not entitled to anything; and if he work with such permission, he has whatever may be agreed upon; and it is alike whether he find in *Ooshree* or *Khirajee* land. (*Moheet-oos-*

[1] This is a branch of the *Zukat*, though restricted at the present day to the following special objects; viz., orphans, the poor, and travellers. *Futawa Alumgeeree*, vol. i. p. 268.

[2] Arab. *Muadin*, pl. of *mâdin*, literally a resting place, from a verb that signifies to *stay*, or to be always in a place.

[3] Arab. *Moontuba*, literally *tractable or yielding.*

[4] Arab. *maee*, from *ma*, water.

[5] The authority for this is the answer of the prophet when asked as to treasure found in the *Adee* war. "Upon it," (said he) and "upon *rikaz* there is a fifth." From his conjoining *rikaz* to something buried in the earth, it is inferred that he meant by it *mâdin*, or things deposited by nature, as well as those concealed by man. The primary signification of *rikaz* is *establishing*, and it is even more applicable to things established by nature in the earth, as component parts of the soil, than to things casually deposited in it.

[6] Arab. *akhiz*, which may either be the proprietor or a casual finder, according as the mine or treasure is found in owned or unowned land.

Surukhsee.) When two men work together in the search for treasure,[1] and one of them lights upon it, it belongs to the actual finder; but when a person hires labourers to work in a mine, the hirer is entitled to whatever may be found. (*Buhr-oor-Raik*). With regard to fluid products, they are such as bitumen or pitch, naphtha, and salt. And those that are neither fusible nor fluid, are such as quicklime, plaster, jewels, and *yakoots*,[2] upon which nothing is due.[3] (*Tuhzeeb.*) On quicksilver a fifth is due. (*Moheet-oos-Surukhsee.*) Fluid products. Minerals.

Nothing is due, according to Aboo Huneefa, on a mine that one finds in his own mansion, and his own land;[4] but the other two have said that something is due.[5] (*Tubyeen*).

[1] The original word here is *rikaz*, and it includes both natural and artificial deposits, as already mentioned.

[2] The *yakoot* comprehends, I think, the ruby, sapphire, and oriental topaz.

[3] The authority is limited to the products that are neither fusible nor fluid, though, I think, intended by the compilers to cover those that are naturally fluid; and it is expressly stated in the *Kifayah* (on the authority of the *Eezah*,) that nothing is due upon them, because they are like water, (vol. i. p. 521). The same doctrine is stated in the *Hidayah*, but it seems limited to fountains of bitumen or pitch, &c., in *Ooshree* land. (*Translation*, vol. i. p. 52).

[4] Aboo Huneefa's opinion is here given without any qualification, but it seems from the *Hidayah*, (*Translation*, vol. i. p. 41,) that there are contradictory reports of it so far as relates to a mine found in one's land. The reason why he may have distinguished between such a mine, and one found within the precincts of a mansion, is thus stated in the *Kifayah*, (vol. i. p. 523.) "When the Imam gives a man his mansion, he gives it to him quite clear, cutting off all others from any participation in it; but this is not the case with land, for when land is given, it is not absolutely cleared from the rights of all others, the *Khiraj* being, in fact, imposed upon it."

[5] That is, a fifth is due, and their opinion seems to be the law; for it is said in the *Hidayah* that a fifth is due on a mine of gold, silver, &c., whether found in *Khirajee* or *Ooshree* land. (*Translation*, vol. i. p. 39.) Nothing is said of the remaining four-fifths; but the whole being constituent parts of the soil, there is no doubt that they belong to the proprietor. Mines and minerals are accordingly included in a sale of land, and pass to the purchaser without special mention. *Moohummudan Law of Sale*, (*Baillie*,) p. 54.

Buried treasure in unowned land.

If a person should find buried treasure[1] within the Mooslim territory, in land that does not belong to any one, as for instance, in an extensive desert, without water; and if it bear the impression of a Mussulman people, as for instance, a legend bearing testimony to the faith, it is to be treated as trove,[2] but if it bear the impress of the people of ignorance,[3] as for instance, if it consist of *dirhems* bearing the sign of the cross, or the figure of an idol, a fifth is due upon it, and the remaining four-fifths belong to the finder. (*Moheet-oos-Surukhsee.*) And if there be any doubt as to the coinage, from there being no sign impressed upon it, it is to be accounted *jahilee*, or of the times of ignorance. (*Kafee.*) It makes no difference whether the finder be a minor or adult, free or a slave, Mooslim or a *Zimmee*; but if he be an alien *Moostamin*, nothing is to be given to him unless he work with the Imam's permission, under a condition for a proportionate division of the profits, in which case, he would be bound to render according to the conditions. (*Moheet.*) And if the finding take place in land that is owned by some one, all are agreed that it is liable to a fifth, but they differ as to the remaining four-fifths; Aboo Huneefa and Moohummud being of opinion that they belong to the original grantee.[4] (*Shurih Tahavee*). And it is stated in the *Futawa Atabeeah*, that if the original grantee were a *Zimmee*, he would not be entitled to anything; but if it be not known who was the original grantee, or if there be no heirs of the original grantee, the four-fifths are to be considered as belonging to the nearest known proprietor, being a Mooslim; (*Tatar Khaneeah,*) or his heirs; (*Buhr-oor-Raik* and *Shurih Taha-*

In proprietary land.

[1] Arab. *Kunz*, which is strictly limited to artificial deposits.

[2] After being duly advertised, if no owner appears, it should be applied in charity, or paid into the *Beit-ool-mal*. See *ante*, p. 12, note 5.

[3] All people not Mahomedan.

[4] Called the *Sahib-ool-Khuttut*, or *Mookhuttut-le-hoo*; the person on whom the Imam bestowed the land originally, at the period of subjugation. (*Hamilton's Hedaya*, vol. i. p. 42.) It is to be observed that concealed treasures are not included in a sale of land, and do not pass to the purchaser. *Moohummudan Law of Sale*, p. 53.

vee;) or failing these, to the *Beit-ool-Mal.* (*Moheet-oor-Surukhsee.*)

If a Mooslim should find buried treasure,[1] or a mine in an enemy's country, in land not owned by any one, it belongs to the finder, and no fifth is due for it; but if he find it in land, the property of an individual among them, and if he entered into their territory under protection, he should restore it to them. Suppose, however, that he does not restore it, but brings it out with him into the Mooslim territory, in that case he is indeed the proprietor of it, but cannot lawfully turn it to his own account; and if he should sell it the purchaser would be under a like disability (*Shurih Tahavee*). The proper course would be to lay it out in charity. (*Buhr-oor-Raik*). But if he had entered the territory without permission, the whole is his own without even the deduction of a fifth (*Mooheet-oos-Surukhsee*).

Treasure or a mine found by a Mooslim in an enemy's country.

Armour, instruments, household goods, stones of rings, and merchandize are in this respect like buried treasure;[2] insomuch that they are liable to a fifth. (*Tubyeen.*)

Armour, instruments, &c. like buried treasure.

There is nothing due upon what may be taken out of the sea, as ambergris, pearls, and fish. (*Futawa Kazee Khan.*) Nor is there a fifth on turquoise stones found in the mountains. (*Hidayah.*)[3]

Things taken out of the sea not liable to any duty.

[1] *Rikaz.* [2] *Kunz.*

[3] See *Translation*, vol. i. p. 43. The reason assigned is the saying of the Prophet, "There is no *khooms* on stones."

CHAPTER V.

OF THE CULTIVATION OF WASTE LANDS.[1]

[This Chapter, with the included Section, forms one entire Book in the *Futawa Alumgeeree*, vol. v. p. 574.]

Description of waste.

Dead or waste land, is land on the outside of a town,[2] for which there is no owner, nor any one who has a particular right in it. What is situated within a town cannot, then, be waste; and in like manner, land on the outside of a town, if it be of use or advantage to the inhabitants, in supplying them with wood or pasturage, is not waste; insomuch that the Imam has not the power of cutting it off. And in the same manner, salt or pitch lands, or the like, which are indispensable to Mahomedans, are not waste, and the Imam cannot lawfully cut them off in favour of any person in particular. But is it a necessary condition, that it shall be distant from cultivated land? Tahavee has made this a condition, but it is not so in the *Zahir Rewayut*, so that a sea near a town, the waters of which have subsided, or a great marsh, the waters of which have subsided, and which has no owner, would be waste according to the *Zahir Rewayut*, but not so,

[1] Arab. *Ihya-ool-muwat.* Literally, giving life to the dead. The figure is too strong for frequent repetition in the English language, and the word "cultivating" does not always indicate the operation intended, as will be seen from the definition given a little further on. As that which is dead is supposed to have lived at one time, the word "reclaiming," which is sometimes applied to the recovery of land from a state of waste, seems to me to render the meaning of the general phrase, as well as could be done by a more literal translation of it. I will, therefore, generally make use of this word as better suited to the act of reducing waste to a state of property.

[2] From *buludu*, he abode in or made his residence.

according to a report of Aboo Yoosuff, on which the opinion of Tahavee is founded. If then, waste be a name for what is of no use, land which has no owner, and in which no one has any particular right, and which is of no use, is waste, whether it be distant from a town not. (*Budayah.*) Qoodooree has said that what is *Adee*,[1] or has been long desolate, and is without a proprietor, or if it ever was appropriated within the time of *Islam*, its owner is unknown,[2] and the land itself lies at such a distance from any village, that if a person were to stand on the nearest limit of cultivated land, and cry out, his voice would not be heard in it, is waste; and *Kazee Fakhr-ood-deen* has said, that what has been said is most correct, that when a man, standing on the verge of the cultivated land of a village, cries out at the pitch of his voice, whatever place his voice reaches to is to be considered as within the confines[3] of the cultivated land, because the people of the village have need of so much for pasture to their cattle, and for other purposes, and that what is beyond this is waste, when it has no known owner. Aboo Yoosuf has made distance from a village, to be determined as aforesaid, a necessary condition; but, according to Moohummud, regard is to be had to the actual fact whether the people of the village derive any advantage from the land or not, though it should be near to the village; but Shums-ool-Aïmmah relies on what was approved by Aboo Yoosuf. (*Kafee.*)

The Imam has the power of cutting off waste; and if he The Imam's

[1] Literally, related to *Aád.* "The tribe of Aád were a race of ancient Arabs, who, according to the Kooran and Arab historians, were destroyed by a suffocating wind, for their infidelity, after their rejection of the admonition of the prophet Hood." *Mr. Lane's Notes to the Arabian Nights Entertainments*, vol. i. p. 131. The word *Adee* is not taken in its literal sense, as related to *Aád* but as merely meaning "what has been long spoiled or desolate." The expression is taken from the saying of the Prophet, "*Adee* land belongs to God and his Prophet, and whoever revives dead land, it is his," and is applied proverbially to anything long gone by, which is said to be of the time of *Aád. Kifayah*, vol. iv. p. 1093.

[2] Land, the owner of which is unknown, is the property of the general body of Mooslims. *Ibid.*

[3] Arab. *fina*, literally "round about," as explained in the *Soorah.*

power to dispose of it.

should do so in favour of a particular individual, and the person should abandon and not cultivate it, no objection will be taken for three years; but when three years have passed, the land returns to the state of waste, and the Ímam may grant it to another. (*Budayah.*)

Property in waste is established by reclaiming it,

Property in waste is established by reclaiming it,[1] with the permission of the Imam according to Aboo Huneefa, and by the mere act of reclaiming, according to Aboo Yoosuf, and Moohummud; and a *Zimmee* becomes the proprietor by reclaiming, in the same way as a Mooslim would acquire the property. (*Budayah.*) A person who reclaims waste land without the permission of the Imam does not become its proprietor according to Aboo Huneefa, but both his companions have said that he does become its proprietor.[2] And Natifee has mentioned, that the *Kazee* within his jurisdiction is in the place of the Imam in this matter. (*Futawa Kazee Khan.*)

and is not lost by subsequent abandonment,

If a person, after reclaiming, should abandon land, and another person should then sow it, it has been said that the second person would have the better right; but the sounder opinion is in favour of the first, for he has become the proprietor by reclaiming it, and will not be expelled from his property by abandoning it.[3]

[1] Arab. *Ihya;* see *ante*, page 40, note 1, and definition a little further on.

[2] Their opinion is founded on the saying of the prophet already quoted, "whoever gives life to dead land it is his," and also on the fact that waste is *Mobah*, or indifferent and free to all. It is therefore the property of the first person who lays his hand upon it, while Aboo Huneefa thinks that the saying alluded to had reference to a particular occasion, and was not intended to establish the law, and that it is opposed to the more general saying of the same person, "There is nothing to man unless what the Imam has consented to." Moreover, waste land having come within the power of Mooslims by aid of horse and spur, is plunder, and, like other plunder, cannot be appropriated by any one without the Imam's permission. *Hidayah and Kifayah*, vol. iv. p. 1093. *Hamilton's Hedaya*, vol. iv. p. 129. When Aboo Yoosuf and Moohummud concur in opinion against Aboo Huneefa, the Moohummudan judge is at liberty to adopt whichever of the decisions he may think more conformable to sound reason and authority. See *Moohum. Law of Sale*, (*Baillie*,) Introduction, p. 55.

[3] The principle of this difference is a difference of opinion as

A person does not acquire a right to waste land by putting a stone upon it,[1] for that in truth is not reclaiming it, which implies the making it fit for sowing, while puting a stone upon it is only marking it by the stone; nor by cutting the grass or thorns that may be upon it; nor by clearing it of any things with which it may be covered, and placing them around the land; nor by burning the thorns, &c. All this does not amount to the establishment of property, but the person who does them has a preferable claim, and the land will not be taken from him for three years, and it would be improper for any other to reclaim this land till three years have expired; but this, rather as a matter of conscience than of law, for if another person should actually reclaim the land before the expiration of three years, he would become the proprietor of it. (*Tibyeen.*)

Acts which do not amount to reclaiming waste land.

A person has placed stones upon a piece of waste land in the form of a minaret; by so doing he has in fact reclaimed it, for that is tantamount to building upon it; and if he should fence it or raise banks so as to retain its water, that would be reclaiming it. (*Mooheet-oos-Surukhsee.*)

Acts which do.

The definition of reclaiming is to build upon land, or plant in it, or plough or water it.[2] (*Khoolasa.*)

Reclaiming defined

The lands of Ma-wura-oon-nuhr[3] and Khwarezm are not waste, for they were once divided,[4] and the disposal of them

Ma-wura-oon-nuhr and Khwa-

to what is acquired by reclaiming land, some being of opinion (among whom was Aboo Kasim, of Bulkh), that it is only a right to the productive power of the land that is acquired, while the general body of the learned maintain that is a right to the land itself. *Kifayah*, vol. iv. p. 1094.

[1] Arab. *tuhjeer*, from *hujur*, a stone.

[2] It appears from the disjunctive *or*, that each act singly is sufficient, but it is stated in the *Hidayah*, (vol. iv. p. 1096,) with regard to ploughing and watering, that one of them singly without the other would not be sufficient, according to Moohummud; but the author of the *Kifayah*, on the passage, cites the *Mubsoot* and the *Zukheerah* as authority, that ploughing or making a mound to retain water, &c., is reclaiming the land, vol. iv. p. 1096; what is meant by watering land is explained a little further on.

[3] What is beyond the river; viz. Transoxiana.

[4] The author seems to have written after the conquest of Jenghiz Khan (about 1221, A.D.,) by which what had been the

rizm, not waste.

belongs to the nearest proprietor or vendor of them, within the time of *Islam*, or his heir; and if he cannot be ascertained, the disposal of them rests with the judge.[1] (*Wujeez-ool-Kurdery.*)

Nor other land which was once appropriated.

Land which has been once appropriated, but the proprietors of which have become extinct, is like trove,[2] but it has been said that it is as waste. (*Zukheerah*). And if a person should erect a building upon it, or sow seed in it, or make for it a dyke or embankment for confining its waters, or the like, the place on which he has built or sown will be his, but no more. Aboo Yoosuf has said, that if he cultivate more than half, that is a reclaiming of so much, and of the remainder also, regard being had to the larger portion.[3] (*Moheet-oos-Surukhsee*). And Moohummud has said that if there be waste in the midst of what has been reclaimed, it is a reclaiming of the whole, but that if the waste be on the side, it is not a reclaiming of what remains. (*Tatar Khaneeah.*) And Ibn Sumaut has related, as from Aboo Huneefa, that if one should dig a well in it, or impel water to it, he has already, in fact, reclaimed it, whether he sow it or not; but though he should dig channels in it, that would not be reclaiming, unless he caused water to flow into them, which also would be reclaiming, but if he were to burn the grass upon it, that would not be reclaiming. (*Moheet-oos-Surukh-*

Dar-ool-Islam, or mansion of Islam, became a *Dar-ool-hurb*, or mansion of the enemy, and before the conversion of his descendant to the Mooslim faith (1348, A.D.,) which restored the country to its former condition.

[1] *Hakim*, from *hookm*, command. The term is also applied to a ruler.

[2] A trove, after being duly advertised, may be kept by the finder indefinitely, until the owner appears; but this seems hardly applicable to land, and land of which the owner is dead, without heirs, belongs to the general body of Mooslims. *Kifayah*, vol. iv. p. 1093.

[3] This extract, though from a different author, evidently relates to the same subject as the former, that is, land once appropriated; but from the former part of the extract, it appears that, generally, nothing more is acquired by reclaiming land, than the actual site or spot reclaimed.

see.) If it were a marsh or forest, and one had cut its reeds or trees, and had levelled the ground, that would be reclaiming it. (*Ghyaseeah.*)

When land is reclaimed by an agent, the principal is the proprietor.

A man has appointed an agent to reclaim land for him, and he has relaimed it; it belongs to the principal, if the Imam gave his permission to reclaim it. (*Koonyah.*)

Land near to land already cultivated cannot be reclaimed.

It is not lawful, according to us, to reclaim what is near to cultivated land. (*Kunz.*)

When the deserted bed of a river, is waste.

What the Tigris or Euphrates has abandoned by recession of their waters, it is not lawful to reclaim, if the water may return to it, because it is necessary to the public to have it as a channel; but if the water cannot return to it, it is waste. (*Siraj-ool-Wuhhaj.*) Land has been submerged and become sea, but the water has again receded from it; or land has been spoiled in any other way, and a person comes and cultivates it; it has been said that the land belongs to the ancient owner, but it has also been said that it belongs to the person who reclaims it. (*Koonyah.*) The Imam has directed a person to cultivate dead land, on condition that he will have advantage from it, but will not be its proprietor, and he has reclaimed it; he is not the proprietor, for this condition is valid, according to Aboo Huneefa, because, in his opinion, the property is not acquired without the Imam's permission, and since the Imam did not give permission to take the property, he does not become its proprietor. (*Moozmirat.*)

Case of land once submerged and again recovered from the sea.

A road to reclaimed land may be made through surrounding land, subsequently reclaimed.

A person reclaimed waste land, and another person then came, and reclaimed all the surrounding land, so as to inclose the land first reclaimed, on its four sides; the first was at liberty to make a road to his land, through the land which the other had reclaimed; and if four persons should come, and each of them should reclaim a side of his land, so as to enclose his land with theirs, he would be at liberty to make a road to his own land, through the land of any of the others he might choose, since they reclaimed the land on his sides together. (*Zuheereeah.*)

Right to a

If a person should dig a well in waste land to such a

well in waste land acquired by digging to within a cubit of water.

depth as to leave but a cubit between him and the water, and another should then dig, the first would have the preferable right in it, unless it were known that he had actually abandoned it, and a month had intervened since he left off; but if he had dug only to the depth of a cubit, that would be no more than marking it, and not reclaiming it. (*Ghyaseeah.*)

When the banks of a great river may be reclaimed.

When there is a river, like the Tigris, with a place for wood or pasturage on its banks, it belongs to him who reclaims it, unless it be within the confines of a village, and the environs would be spoiled thereby; in which case he will be prevented, and the governor of a country may cut off[1] a part from the line of the highway, when not injurious to the Mooslims; but some say that this power belongs only to the *Khuleef*, and those to whom he may specially commit it. (*Moheet.*)

When the side of the highway.

Incidents of waste.

There are two effects or consequences that result from the reclaiming of waste. One of these is *hureem*[2] and the other *Wuzeefa.*

1. *Hureem.*

With regard to the first there are two points for consideration, one of which has relation to the right to *hureem*, and the other to its extent. Now as regards the right, there is no difference of opinion, that if a man should dig a well in waste land, he has a *hureem* to it, and can prevent another from digging within its *hureem*. In like manner, a spring or fountain has its *hureem*, according to all opinions. As regards its extent, the *hureem* of a spring is 500 *ziras* by common consent.[3] (*Budayah.*) It has been said, that it is

Of a spring

[1] That is, in favour of an individual.

[2] Literally, *forbidden*.

[3] The authority for this is the saying of the Prophet, "The *hureem* of a spring is 500 *ziras.*" *Hidayah*, vol. iv. p. 1096. It will be seen presently that the *hureem* of a well is only forty or sixty *ziras* at the most, and it is natural to inquire what is the reason of so great a difference, and how is a spring or fountain distinguished from a well? The spring or fountain is brought out to water the ground, and one space is required through which the water may be conducted from the fountain, another for a reservoir wherein the water may be collected; and a third for

500 *ziras* on the four sides taken together, that is 125 *ziras* on each side; but the more correct opinion is, that it is 500 *ziras* on each side; and the *zira* intended is the *mookussur*, or shortened *zira*, of six hands.[1] (*Tibyeen.*) The *hureem* of a well which can be drawn by the hand is forty *ziras*,[2] (*Bidayah*); and here also it has been said that it is forty *ziras* on the four sides together, that is only ten on each side; but the correct opinion is, that it is forty *ziras* on each side. (*Tibyeen*). The *hureem* of a well which requires camels to draw it,[3] is sixty *ziras*, according to the two; but Aboo Huneefa has said "I know only forty *ziras*," and the *Futwa* is with him.[4] Sudur-oos-Shuheed has related, that if a person should open a channel in waste land, he would not, in the opinion of Aboo Huneefa, according to some, have any right to a *hureem*, and that according to the other two he would have a right to it; but what is correct is, that he would be entitled to a *hureem*, according to all their opinions. And it is stated in the *Nuwazir* that the *hureem* of a water-course is half its breadth on each side, according to Aboo

Of a well.

Of a water course.

conveying the water from the reservoir to moisten the lands. *Hamilton's Hedaya*, vol. iv. p. 135. A spring, therefore, rises to the surface and flows off, while the water remains in the well till it is drawn off.

[1] The ordinary *zira* was a hand more.

[2] The authority for this is the saying of the Prophet, "He who digs a well has around it forty *ziras* as an *utun* for his beasts." *Hidayah*, vol. iv. p. 1096. *Utun* means literally *a reclining place for camels*, but an *utun* well is described in the *Kifayah* as one that can be drawn by the hand, as if all the space required is room for the camels to lie down.

[3] Arab. *Nazih*, a camel that draws water, hence the well is called a *nazih* well. The opinion of the two is founded on the express saying of the Prophet, viz. "The *hureem* of a spring is 500 *ziras*, the *hureem* of an *utun* well is forty *ziras*, and the *hureem* of a *nazih* well is sixty *ziras*," while Aboo Huneefa rests on the saying already quoted, where there is no distinction as to a *nazih* well, and a general saying which all agree in accepting and acting upon, is preferable in his opinion to a special saying which men differ in accepting and acting upon. *Hidayah* and *Kifayah*, vol. iv. p. 1096.

[4] No authority is cited, unless it be considered as part of the following sentences.

Yoosuf, and the full breadth on each side according to Mohummud; but the *Futwa* is according to the saying of Aboo Yoosuf. (*Futawa Kazee Khan.*)

2. *Wuzeefa.*

The second effect or consequence of reclaiming waste land is liability to *Wuzeefa;* and if a Mooslim should reclaim it, Aboo Yoosuf has said that the land would be *Ooshree* if contiguous to *Ooshree* land, and *Khirajee* if contiguous to *Khirajee* land; while Moohummud has said that if he reclaim it by means of *Ooshr* water it is *Ooshree*, and if he reclaim it by means of *Khiraj* water, it is *Khirajee;* but if a *Zimmee* should reclaim it, it would be *Khirajee* under all circumstances, according to all opinions. (*Budayah.*)

No one can lawfully dig a well in the *hureem* of another.

When a person has dug a well in a desert, with permission of the Imam, and another then comes and digs a well within its *hureem*, the first may close up what the second has dug; and in like manner, if another should build, or sow, or innovate upon it in any way, the first may prevent him, by reason of his right of property in the place. But if we suppose that another, by order of the Imam, should dig a well not within the *hureem* of the first, though near to it, and that the water should go away from the well of the first, and it is manifest that this has been occasioned by the digging of the second well, the digger of the second would not be in any way responsible to the owner of the first. (*Mubsoot.*)

Qualification of the right to *hureem.*

The right of *hureem*, extending on all sides into waste land, is subject to this qualification, that it is only in land to which no one has any right; for if one person should dig a well, and another should then come and dig a well on the verge of his *hureem*, the second would have no right to a *hureem* on that side where lay the *hureem* of the first, though he would be entitled to it on the other sides, where it would not interfere with the right of another person. (*Nihayah.*)

Hureem of a tree.

When a man has planted a tree, with the permission of the Imam, according to the three, or without it, according to the two, has he a right to a *hureem* for it, so that if another should come and plant a tree by the side of his tree, could he prevent him? Moohummud has not adverted to this case in his book; but our Elders have said that he has a right to the extent of five *ziras.* (*Moheet.*)

No *hureem* to a palace.

A man erects a palace in the desert; but he has no right to a *hureem,* though it should be required for casting out rubbish; for he can derive the benefit of his palace without having a *hureem.* (*Tibyeen.*)

SECTION.

Of the Digging or Clearing of Water Courses and Repairing them.

Water courses are of three kinds.

Water-courses are of three kinds. Of some the digging is on the Sooltan; of others, the digging is on the proprietors of the water-course, and they may be compelled to dig if they refuse; of the third, the digging is also on the proprietors, but they cannot be compelled, if they refuse.

1. The great, or public rivers.

The first are the great rivers, which have never entered into division, such as the Euphrates, the Tigris, Jyhoon, Syhoon, and the Nile, which is a river of Room.[1] When these require to be dug, or their banks to be repaired, it will be done by the Sooltan out of the public treasury, and if there be no funds in the public treasury, the Mooslims will be compelled to dig, and turn out for this purpose. If an individual Mooslim should wish to dig a channel from these for the purpose of watering his lands, he may do so, when it will not be injurious to the public; but if it would be injurious to the public, by breaking the bank, or there should be any apprehension of inundation, he will be prevented.

2. General rivers.

The second, or those water-courses the clearing and repairing of which is the duty of their owners, and which, if they refuse, they will be compelled by the Imam to perform,

[1] These rivers are said to be public in every sense; their waters never have been divided, and never can be divided, because one day they belong to one nation, and the next to others; that is, I suppose, their courses stretch through different countries. See *Kifayah*, vol. iv. p. 1105.

are large rivers which have entered into division or distribution among villages.[1] The clearing and repairing of these, when required, is upon their owners, and when they refuse, they are to be compelled; for a neglect of this duty redounds to the injury of the whole,[2] and may diminish the supply of water to those who are entitled to it, for drink to themselves and cattle,[3] as well as lead to a scarcity of grain. Since then the proprietors have the benefit of the water, and the injury from a neglect of digging falls upon the whole, they may be compelled to dig.[4] From these rivers no one has a right to cut a channel to water his own land, whether that would injure the owners of the stream or not. In this water there is no right of *shoofa.*[5]

3. Private rivers.

The third, or those water-courses the clearing and repairing of which is the duty of their owners, but which they cannot be compelled to clear and repair, are private rivers. With regard to these, some say that if a river belong to ten or fewer persons,[6] or there be only one village upon it, to which its waters are divided, it is a private river, which is

[1] These are said to be public in one sense, and private in another. *Kifayah*, vol. iv. p. 1105. The former, probably, from the greater number of persons who are entitled to share in their waters.

[2] That is, the remaining partners. *Hidayah*, vol. iv. p. 1106.

[3] Arab. *Ahl-oos-Shooft*, or people of *shooft*, *shooft* being the right to water for drink to man and beast, common to all mankind. It may be observed, that the diminution of this supply is not a reason why the proprietors can be compelled to dig, for there is no compulsion on this account. *Ibid.* page 1107.

[4] That is, each individual may be compelled to dig, because he is benefitted, and his neglect would injure, not himself only, but the whole body of proprietors.

[5] Pre-emption. In the original the word is *shooft* not *shoofa*, but I think this must be a misprint, for it appears from what is said above that there is a common right of *shooft* in the waters of these rivers, and further, there is no other allusion to the right of *shoofa*, though the absence of that right in these rivers, and its existence in the next class, is that which mainly distinguishes the one from the other.

[6] I have added the word *persons*, believing that to be intended, though in the original the words are only "ten or more," and so in the other cases. It is important, that however great the number of persons, if there be only one village upon the river, it is private.

subject to the right of *Shoofa*.[1] Some say again, that if it belong to fewer than forty persons it is a private river, and that if it belong to forty it is general; while others say that if the number be under a hundred it is private; and others that if it be under a thousand it is private; but what has been said, that it ought to be committed to a *Moojtuhid* or scientific jurist to choose among these sayings, is the most correct. With regard then to private rivers, if some of the partners should wish to clear them and others refuse, Aboo Bukr Ben Saeed of Balkh has said, that the Imam will not compel them, and that if those who wish that they should be cleared, should proceed to clear them, they would be voluntaries in the matter; but Aboo Bukr-al-Askaf has said that they will be compelled, and Khusaf has stated, in treating of maintenance, that the *Kazee* will direct those who desire the clearance of the channel, to clear it, and when they have done this, they may prohibit the others from deriving any advantage from it, until they contribute their shares of the expense of clearing; and to this effect there is a report from Aboo Yoosuf. If the whole of them wish to abandon the digging, the Imam will not compel them, according to the *Zahir Rewayut;* but some of the moderns have said that the Imam will compel them. (*Futawa Kazee Khan.*)[2]

[1] See before, note 5. "The difference between them (that is the two last classes) is the right to *shoofa*, and the absence of that right, that is, wherever there is the right, the river is private, wherever it is not, it is general. *Kifayah*, vol. iv. p. 1106.

[2] The authority seems to apply to the whole of this section.

CHAPTER VI.

OF MOOZARAUT.[1]

[This Chapter is composed of extracts from the Book of *Moozâraût*. *Futawa Alumgeeree*, vol. v. p. 359.]

Legal character. It is invalid, according to Aboo Huneefa, but permitted according to the other two; and the *Futwa* is in accordance with their opinion, from a regard to the necessities of mankind. Definition. In law it is defined to be a contract of sowing for some part of the produce; and it is a hiring, either of the land, or of the labourer,[2] for a part of the produce. (*Moheet-oos-Surukhsee.*) How constituted. It is constituted by declaration and acceptance; that is, if the owner of the land[3] say to the labourer, "I have delivered to thee this land in *Moozâraût* for so much," and the labourer say, "I have accepted," or "am satisfied," or what indicates his acceptance or satisfaction; when this has taken place, the contract between them is perfected.

Conditions. The conditions of the contract, according to those who approve of it, are of two kinds, confirmatory and invalidating. Confirmatory. The confirmatory conditions are also of several kinds; some having reference to the parties,[4] some to the instrument of

[1] Infinitive of the fifth increased conjugation, from *zurau*, sowing. It means, literally, "mutual sowing," or "mutual cultivation," which would require the action of both parties to the contract, whereas, in law, the action is entirely on one side. *Kifayah*, vol. iv. p. 996.

[2] Arab. *Amil.* from *uml*, work.

[3] Arab. *Sahib-ool-urz.* See *ante*, p. 11, note 2.

[4] Arab. *Moozârea*, participle of the fifth increased conjugation, strictly applicable to both parties to the contract, and so evidently applied here, and a little further on, but usually restricted to the labourer or husbandman. It is worthy of remark, that it is used

Moozâraüt, some to the thing sown, some to the issue from the sowing, some to the place in which it is sown, and some to the time of the contract.

That relate to the parties.

There are two conditions that relate to the parties. The first is, that they be persons of understanding; and the *Moozâraüt* of an insane person, or of a youth who does not understand *Moozâraüt*, is invalid. The second is that they should not be apostates, according to those who follow the analogy of Aboo Huneefa's opinion, yet approve of *Moozâraüt*;[1] but according to the other two, this is not a condition necessary to the legality of *Moozâraüt*, and the *Moozâraüt* of an apostate is immediately operative.

—the thing sown.

With regard to the thing sown, or the species of seed, it is requisite that it should be known; by which is meant, that it should be explained, unless the labourer be told to sow what he pleases, when he would be at liberty to sow anything, but not to plant, for it is only sowing, not planting, that falls within the scope of the contract. (*Bidayah.*) It is not a condition that the quantity of the seed should be explained, for that may be known by indicating the land; and though the parties should not have explained the kind of seed, yet if the seed were to be supplied by the owner of the land, the contract would be lawful, because with regard to him the *Moozâraüt* is not binding before the casting of the seed, and at the casting of the seed, the point is ascertained, and information, when a contract becomes binding, is equiva-

in this sense, in India. In the address at the head of zemindary *Sunuds*, it occurs in conjunction with *Raaya*, (the plural of Ryot,) thus *Raaya o Moozara-an*, "subjects and cultivators." (*Dissertation on the Landed Property of Bengal, by C. W. B. Rouse*, p. 74.) The first word literally means "herds of cattle," or "beasts of burden," but is applied to subjects generally, or the people at large, more particularly the poorer classes; the latter being a technical term, seems to indicate that the persons to whom it is applied, were, at one time, *Moozârea* in the strict sense of the word, that is, that they held their lands under this particular contract.

[1] That is, those who agree with Aboo Huneefa as to the incompetency of an apostate, yet differ from him in thinking *Moozâraüt* lawful.

lent to information at the time of contracting. (*Futawa Kazee Khan.*)

— the produce.

The conditions that relate to the issue or produce from the sowing, are of several kinds, and among these, it is required that the produce be mentioned at the contract, for silence in regard to it would vitiate the contract; that it shall belong to both the parties, for if the whole be stipulated to one of them, the contract is invalid; that the share of each of the parties[1] shall be a portion of the produce, for if agreed for in anything else, that would vitiate the contract, as being inconsistent with the idea of partnership, which is essential to this contract; that this portion of the produce shall be known in quantity, as a half, a third, a fourth, or the like, and shall be a distributive or indiscriminate share of the whole, for if a known number of *kufeezes* were stipulated for in favour of one of the parties, that would invalidate the contract, and in like manner, if one of the parties should stipulate for a return of the seed, and that the remainder of the produce, after deducting it, should be divided between them, the *Moozâraŭt* would not be valid, as the land might yield no more than a return for the seed.

—the land.

The conditions that relate to the place of sowing, or in other words, the land, are, that it shall be in a state fit for sowing, for if excessively moist the contract is unlawful; that it be known, for if unknown, the *Moozâraŭt* is not valid, as that would lead to contention; that the land should be delivered up to the contractor[2] vacated, that is, that there should be on the part of the owner of the land, a vacating of the land to the labourer; for if it were stipulated that that the landlord[3] should work, the *Moozâraŭt* would not be valid for want of vacating; and in like manner, if it were stipulated that both should work together. (*Bidayah.*) Vacating is when the owner of the land says to the labourer, "I have delivered up to thee the land," and it implies that

1 Literally, the two *Moozarea.*

2 Arab. *Akid*, which is here substituted for *amil.*

3 Arab. *Rubb-ool-urz*, literally, lord or master of the land. The same person is evidently intended as he who has just been called *Sahib-ool-urz*, or owner of the land.

the land is actually vacant or free of anything at the time of the contract; for if it contain seed that has already sprung up, the contract, though lawful, would be a *Mooâmulüt,*[1] not a *Moozâraüt,* and if the seed have become plant that has already ripened, there would no longer be any occasion for work, which would preclude the idea of *Mooâmulüt,* and the contract would be entirely unlawful. (*Futawa Kazee Khan.*)

So far as relates to the instrument of *Moozâraüt,* it is required that the cattle shall be an accessory, for if made a primary object in the contract, that would vitiate the *moozâraut.* —the cattle.

With regard to the time[2] it is necessary that it should be known, and *Moozâraüt* is not valid without an explanation of the time, on account of the difference in the times of commencing the operations of husbandry; but if the transaction take place in a village[3] where there is no such difference, it is lawful, without any specification of the time. (*Bidayah.*) If a time be mentioned which is insufficient for the cultivation, the *Moozâraüt* is vitiated, such mention being equal to no mention at all; and in like manner, when a time is mentioned that there is no probability of one of the parties living so long.[4] (*Zukheerah.*) —the time.

It is further requisite that it should be specified by which of the parties the seed is to be supplied; for if it be supplied by the owner of the land the *Moozâraüt* is a hiring of the labourer, and if it is supplied by the labourer the *Moozâraüt* is a hiring of the land; the subject of the contract therefore, Further requisites as to the seed.

[1] Mutual working, from *uml,* work.

[2] Arab. *mooddut,* from *mudd,* extension—a space of time. From the examples, it is evident that the beginning and the end of the time should be known.

[3] Arab. *Mowzah.* This is the common name for a village in India.

[4] The time should be limited, as " for one or two years, or the like." But Moohummud Ben Sulma has said that *Moozâraüt* without any limit of time is lawful, and that in that case, it will be presumed to be for one year, or for one sowing. *Kifayah,* vol. iv. p. 995. A case is mentioned in the *Khuzanut-ool-Mooftien,* of a *Moozâraüt* for three years. *Fut. Alum.* vol. v. p. 379.

is unknown. Its effects also are different; for the contract with regard to him by whom the seed is not to be supplied is immediately binding, but with regard to the owner of the seed, it is not binding till the seed is cast into the ground. The lawyer Aboo Bukr, of Bulkh, has said, that custom is the rule in this case; if the transaction take place in a village where the seed is usually supplied by the labourer or by the owner of the land, regard is to be had to the custom of the people, and the party who would be liable to furnish the seed according to the custom, should be made to supply it, if the practice be uniform, but if in both ways, the *Moozâraŭt* would be invalid. This is when no words are used to indicate the party by whom the seed is to be supplied; but if the owner of the land should say, "I have delivered to thee this land that thou mayest sow it for me," or "I have hired thee to work in it for half the produce;" this would amount to an indication that the seed was to be supplied by the owner of the land; while if he should say, "that thou mayest sow it for thyself," it would indicate that the seed was to be supplied by the labourer. (*Futawa Kazee Khan*). And Ibn Roostum has reported, as from Moohummud, in his *Nuwadir*, that if one person should say to another, "I have let thee this my land for a year, at a half," or "a third," it would be lawful, and the cultivator be bound to furnish the seed; but suppose him to say, "I have delivered to thee my land in *Moozâraŭt*," or "have given thee my land in *Moozâraŭt* for a third," that would not be lawful, since there is nothing to show by whom the seed is to be supplied, which is a necessary condition; while, if he were to say, "I have hired thee to sow this my land for a third," that would be lawful, and the supply of the seed obligatory on the landlord. (*Zukheerah*).

Invalidating conditions.

The conditions which invalidate *Moozâraŭt* are of different kinds, and among them are the following: viz. a condition that the whole produce shall belong to one of the parties, for that cuts off the idea of a partnership; a condition for work on the part of the owner of the land, for that prevents delivery; a condition that he shall furnish the cattle; a condition that he shall reap the grain, and deliver it at the threshing floor, and tread it out, and sift it. The principle is, that every thing required for the good of the plant previous to its ripening and drying, such as watering, guarding, pulling up grass, digging water courses, and the like, is to be performed by the cultivator, and every work that may be required between the ripening and drying of the crop, and the partition of the grain, for the purposes of separating it from the husk, and winnowing it, is to be performed by both the parties, in proportion to their interests in the produce, and every work which may be required after partition, for the purpose of carrying the grain to the house, and securing it, is to be done by each party in relation to his own portion. And it is reported of Aboo Yoosuf that he sanctioned a condition imposing on the cultivator the duty of reaping, and delivering the grain at the threshing floor, and treading it out and sifting it, from a regard to the practice of mankind; and some of our Doctors in Mawura-oon-nuhr have decided accordingly. Nusr Ben Yahya and Moohummud Ben Soolma, among those of Khoorassan, also approving of the decision. (*Bidayah.*) But such a condition, imposing these duties on the labourer, would be unlawful, according to the *Zahir Rewayut.* (*Futawa Kazee Khan and Koobra.*) While Nusr Ben Yahya and Moohummud Ben Soolma have said that all this must be done by the labourer, whether conditioned for or not, from a regard to custom, and according to *Surukhsee* this is correct in our country, and Aboo Bukr Ben Moohummud, when asked his opinion upon the point, used to answer, that the practice was quite clear. (*Futawa Kazee Khan.*)

Further conditions that would vitiate the contract.

Among vitiating conditions is also to be mentioned a condition for the straw to one who does not supply the seed, and a condition by the owner of the land as against the cultivator, for some work the effect and advantage of which will continue after the expiration of the time. As to ploughing, if stipulated for absolutely without any mention of its being to be done twice, a stipulation for it would not vitiate the *Moozâraüt*, according to general agreement; and this is correct; but if the parties should agree that it is to be done twice, that would vitiate the *Moozâraût;* for by twice must be meant, either that one of the ploughings is to be before the sowing, and the other after the reaping, in order that the land may be returned ploughed to the owner, which would, without doubt, vitiate the contract, for ploughing after the harvest is not an operation of the same year; or that the land is to be ploughed twice before it is sown, which would be a work that must leave its effect and advantage after the expiration of the term; and such a condition would vitiate the contract, except in a *mouzah* or village, where there would be no such continuance of the advantage.

Effects of *Moozâraût.*

Among the effects or consequences of *Moozâraût*, are the following. Every act necessary for the good of the plant must be done by the cultivator, and everything necessary for its nourishment, such as dung, the extraction of grass,[1] and the like, must be contributed by both the parties, in proportion to their respective rights. And so also with regard to the reaping, and carrying the produce to the threshing floor, and treading it out. It is a further consequence that the parties are entitled to the produce in the proportions specified, and that when the earth makes no return, neither of them is entitled to anything, either as wages of labour or rent of land, whether the seed have been supplied by the labourer or the owner of the land; (*Bidayah;*) and further, that when any calamity overtakes the plant before ripening, neither party has any claim against his fellow. (*Zukheerah.*) It is a further effect of this contract, that it is not binding on the party who has to furnish the seed, but binding on his fellow, so that if the former, after entering into the contract, should refuse to proceed, saying "I do not wish to sow," he is at liberty to decline, with or without reason, but his fellow cannot decline, without a sufficient reason. (*Bidayah.*) After the seed has been cast into the ground, the contract becomes binding upon both parties; so that after this, one of the parties cannot cancel without an adequate reason. (*Moheet.*) It is stated in the Moontuka, as from Aboo Yoosuf, that when the

[1] This seems inconsistent with what was said on page 57, but the words are the same in the original.

seed is to be furnished by the landlord, and he has delivered it to the cultivator, neither of them has the power to cancel the *Moozâraüt*, but if he has not delivered the seed to the cultivator, the landlord may cancel the contract, but the cultivator has not the power to do so. (*Zukheerah.*) Another effect of the contract is the power of compelling the cultivator to plough. When there is an express stipulation to that effect, he may of course be compelled to plough, and even when there is no such stipulation, yet if the land be such as does not usually yield its produce without ploughing, or only to a small extent, he may be compelled to plough. If, however, the land should be such as usually yields its produce in an adequate degree without ploughing, then he cannot be compelled to plough, in the absence of an express stipulation. And in like manner, if the cultivator should refuse to water, he cannot be compelled when the land is such as usually yields its produce with water from the heavens; but if it be such that the rain from the heavens is not sufficient to enable it to make a suitable return, then he may be compelled to water it. (*Bidayah.*)

Different kinds of *Moozâraüt*.

*With regard to the different kinds of *Moozâraüt*, the principle in these matters is that the hiring of land for a portion of the produce is lawful, and that the hiring of the labourer for a portion of the produce is also lawful, but that the hiring of any other than these for a portion of the produce is not lawful. (*Moheet.*) *Moozâraüt* is of two kinds, one where the land belongs to one of the parties, and the other where it belongs to both. The former case, where the land belongs to one of the parties, is further divided into two kinds; one where the seed belongs to only one of the parties, and the other where it belongs to both. When the land belongs to only one of the parties, and the seed also to only one, the contract admits of six different species, three of which are lawful and three invalid. Of the three first, one species is where the land is supplied by one party, and the seed, the cattle, and labour by the other, and some known

Six species of the contract.

Three lawful.

* N.B. The extracts from hence to the N.B. on page 61, are taken from the second chapter, p. 364-367.

share of the produce is stipulated for to the owner of the land. This is lawful; for the owner of the seed becomes the hirer of the land for a portion of the produce. The second species is, where the labour is supplied by one and the remainder by the other; and this too is lawful, because the owner of the seed is the hirer of the labourer for something known out of the produce, that he may work the land with his cattle and his seed. The third species is when the land and seed are furnished by one party, and the labour and cattle by the other; and this likewise is lawful, for the owner of the land becomes the hirer of the labourer, that the labourer may work with his cattle for the owner of the land and seed.

Three invalid.

Of the invalid species of *Moozâraût* the first is where the land and cattle are supplied by one of the parties, and the remainder by the other; and this is invalid, for though, according to Aboo Yoosuf it is allowed, from a regard to custom, yet the *Futwa* is with the *Zahir Rewayut*, because the advantage derived from the land and from the cattle, are not of the same kind, that of the land being the growth of the seed from a power inherent in it, and that from the cattle being labour, and since the advantage derived from the cattle is not of the same kind as that derived from the land, the cattle cannot be an accessory to the land, but stand as a separate object in the contract, which would thus be a hiring of the cattle, and be defective in the same way as if the cattle alone belonged to one of the parties. The second of the invalid species is where the seed belongs to one of the parties, and all the rest to the other; and this is invalid, because the owner of the seed becomes the hirer of the land, which should be vacated or delivered to him, but it is in the hands of the labourer, not of the owner of the seed. And the third of the species is, where the seed and the cattle belong to one of the parties, and the land and the labour to the other, and this also is invalid.[1] (*Futawa Kazee Khan.*)

[1] It is unnecessary to pursue the subject farther into cases where the seed belongs to both, but the land to only one of the parties, or where the land belongs to both, and the seed also to

Effects of an invalid *Moozâraŭt.*

When a *Moozâraŭt* is invalid, the cultivator is not bound to perform any of the acts which are required of him under a lawful contract; the whole crop belongs to the owner of the seed, whether he be the owner of the land or the cultivator; and when the seed belongs to the owner of the land the cultivator is entitled to the wages of his labour, and when it belongs to the labourer, the landlord is entitled to the hire or rent of his land.[1] (*Bidayah.*)

Miscellaneous cases

* A person delivers land and seed to another, that he may sow it by himself, and with his cattle and hired servants, and the parties agree that the whole produce shall belong to the owner of the land; this transaction is lawful, as stated by Moohummud, in the *Asul;* not however, that it is a lawful *Moozâraŭt,* for such a transaction is not a *Moozâraŭt* at all, since in a *Moozâraŭt* it is necessary that the produce shall be in partnership between both the parties, and here there is no partnership. It is merely meant, that if the whole produce be stipulated for to the owner of the seed, it is lawful. And if it were agreed that the whole produce should belong to the cultivator, that also would be lawful; meaning thereby that a stipulation for the whole of the produce to the cultivator is lawful. (*Zukheerah.*) When a person delivers seed to another, saying, "sow it in thy land, that the whole produce may be thine," or "sow thy land with my seed that the whole produce may be thine;" this is lawful, and the owner of the seed becomes a lender of it to the owner of the land, that he may sow it in his land, the landlord having already possession of it in his hands. But if the owner of the seed had said to him, "sow for me thy land with my seed, and the whole produce shall be thine," this would be invalid, and the whole produce would belong

both of the parties. In some of these cases the contract is lawful, and in others invalid, according to the special stipulations with which it may be accompanied; but they do not seem to have been much in use, and are not mentioned in the *Hidayah.*

[1] There are other effects which it is unnecessary to specify.

* N.B. The authorities from this to the N.B. on page 64, are from chapter iii. p. 367-372.

to the owner of the seed. And when seed is delivered to a man that he may sow it in his land, on condition that the whole produce shall belong to the owner of the seed, such a condition is lawful, and the owner of the seed becomes a borrower of the land from the landlord, availing himself of his assistance to sow it with his seed; all which is lawful. But suppose that he had said, "sow this in thy land for thyself, on condition that what return God may bestow shall be wholly mine;" the whole produce would belong to the owner of the land, and the owner of the seed would be entitled to the return of a similar, in kind and quantity, of his seed. (*Zukheerah.*) And when a man delivers his land to another that he may sow it, on condition that what God may bestow, shall belong to both in halves, but the parties are silent with regard to the obligation to supply the cattle being on the labourer, or it may be that it is made an express condition; the labourer would in both cases be obliged to supply the cattle, whether the seed were on his part or on that of the owner of the land, because the cattle are the instrument of labour, and must be supplied by him who is obliged to provide the labour. (*Khuzanut-ool-Mooftieen.*)

Stipulations for payment of the *Khiraj.*

When the land is *Khirajee*, and the parties make it a condition that the *Khiraj* shall be set apart, and the remainder be divided among them in halves, this is invalid, if the land be *Moowuzzuf*, as it may possibly yield no more than the amount of the *Khiraj;* but if the *Khiraj* be *Mookasimah*, as a third or a fourth, the condition would be lawful. (*Kafee.*) And if there be a stipulation in favour of the owner of the seed for a tenth of the produce, after which the remainder is to be divided between them, the *Moozâraŭt* is lawful; for such a stipulation is not inconsistent with the idea of a partnership in the produce, since, however small the produce may be, there will still be a tenth of it; and this affords a device to the owner of the seed by which he may secure to himself a return of his seed; for he may stipulate in his own favour for a quantity equal to the seed, under the name of a tenth, a third, or the like, and that the remainder, after deducting it, shall be divided between the parties. (*Nihayah.*) If it be stipulated that a tenth shall be to one who does not furnish the seed, and that the remainder shall belong to both the parties, the condition is lawful; and supposing the land to be *Ooshree*, and that the parties should stipulate for setting apart a tenth, if it should be watered by flowing water, or half a tenth if it should be watered by the wheel, and a division of the remainder between them, in halves, that also would be lawful; and when the produce is obtained and the Sooltan has taken his right, either a tenth or half a tenth, as the case may be, the remainder will belong to the parties, in halves. And if the Sooltan should not take anything from them, or they should clandestinely abstract a part of their grain from the Sooltan, the tenth out of this, which was conditioned in favour of the Sooltan, would belong to the owner of the land, according to those who follow the general analogy of Aboo Huneefa's opinion, yet approve of *Moozâraŭt;* but according to Aboo Yoosuf and Moohummud, it would belong to both the parties, in halves. But suppose that his companion should say to the labourer, "I dont know what the Sooltan may take from us, whether a tenth, or half a tenth, but I employ you on condition that half what the land may yield, after deducting what is taken by the Sooltan, shall be mine, and half yours;" that would be invalid, according to the analogy of Aboo Huneefa's opinion, but lawful, according to Aboo Yoosuf and Moohummud, and the division would be between them as agreed upon. The case supposes that the land is such that the water of the heavens would suffice for it when the rains are abundant, but that it requires to be watered by means of the wheel when the rains are deficient, and in taking a tenth or half a tenth from such land, the Sooltan has regard to the greater part of the year.[1] The case is, therefore the same, as if the parties should say, "we dont know how the rain may be this year, and consequently what the Sooltan may take out of the produce," and should enter into their agreement accordingly. Then, according to Aboo Huneefa, as the landlord is liable for a tenth or half a tenth,

or *Ooshr.*

Alternative conditions relating to the *Ooshr.*

[1] See *ante*, page 26.

such a stipulation is equivalent to a condition for an unknown portion, viz. a tenth or half a tenth, in favour of the landlord, which would vitiate the contract; but according to Aboo Yoosuf and Moohummud, the tenth or half tenth is in the produce, and as the produce is between them both in halves, the stipulation is merely a condition that the whole produce shall belong to the parties in halves, which does not vitiate the contract. (*Mubsoot.*) And if the land be *Khirajee*, and the owner of the land should say to the labourer, "we dont know whether the Sooltan will this year take from us *Khiraj Wuzeefa*, or *Khiraj Mookasimah*, by which is meant that the land is really *Wuzeefa*, but that in some years it is unable to pay *Wuzeefa Khiraj*, when it would not be lawful for the Sooltan to take the *Khiraj Wuzeefa*, but he must take it *Mookasimah*,[1] that is, as far as a half of the produce, and that the proprietor[2] in fact says, "we do not know whether the land will this year be able to bear the *Wuzeefa*, in which case the Sooltan would take that, or whether it will not be able to bear it, when he will only take *Mookasimah*," and further says to the *Moozârea*, "I will employ you on condition that whatever the Sooltan may take, be it *Mookasimah* or *Wuzeefa*, shall be deducted, and the remainder be divided between us," such a *Moozâraŭt* would be invalid. And suppose that a person should give up his land to two others to sow it with their seed, on condition that one should have a third of the produce and the other nine *Kufeezes* out of the produce, the *Moozâraŭt* would be vitiated *in toto*, according to him; while with the other two, it would be lawful as to the person to get the third, but invalid with respect to the person for whom nine *Kufeezes* was stipulated. (*Kafee.*)

Alternative conditions in relation to *Khiraj*.

[3] When a cultivator wishes to give up the land to another,

Sub Moozâraŭt unlawful, without

[1] See *ante*, page 6, note 3.

[2] Arab. *Malik*. The word signifies proprietor in the most absolute sense, and being here applied to the *Sahib-ool-Urz*, shews that by that expression is to be understood not the mere possessor, but the actual owner of the land.

[3] The authorities to the N.B. on page 68, are from chapter v. p. 382-385.

in *Moozâraüt*, if the seed were supplied by the landlord, he cannot lawfully give up the land without the landlord's permission, either express or implied, as, for instance, by the landlord's saying, "do with it as you please." He may, however, hire labourers with his own property, to perform the work, unless it were expressly stipulated that he should do the work himself. And if he should give up the land to another, at a half, though the landlord had not given his permission, either expressly or by implication, it has been said that the *Moozâraüt* would be lawful, as between the first and second cultivator, and that the landlord would have nothing, but that the owner of the land and seed might make either of the parties responsible for his seed; and if he should cast the responsibility on the first, the first could have no recourse against the second; while, if the second were made responsible, he might have recourse to the first; but if the land were damaged, the second, and not the first, would be responsible, according to Aboo Huneefa, and the last opinion of Aboo Yoosuf. (*Zukheerah.*)

landlord's permission, when he supplies the seed.

If the owner of the land and seed should give his permission to the cultivator, expressly or by implication, as, for instance, if he should say, "do with it as you please," and if the owner of land and seed had already stipulated with the cultivator for a half, and the first should give up the land to the second, the second *Moozâraüt* would be lawful, but whatever the earth might produce, would belong, one half to the landlord, and one half to the second cultivator, while the first would fall between them; but if the first should stipulate with the second for a half to the owner of the property,[1] and the remaining half either in one

Lawful, with it.

[1] Arab. *Mal*, which includes both land and seed. As this word is commonly applied in India to the land revenue, or the *Khiraj* itself, but has been confounded by some writers with the *right to the Khiraj*, I avail myself of its occurrence in this place to explain what I believe to be its strict meaning in the Moohummudan Law, though I may, perhaps, be led beyond the ordinary limits of a foot note. *Mal*, or property, is defined to be "that which can be taken possession of and secured." (*Hidayah* and *Kifayah*, vol. iii. p. 103.) It is, therefore, essentially tangible or corporeal; and a mere right cannot, in any sense, be said to be

and two thirds, or in halves, between the cultivators, that also would be lawful, and the produce be divided, according as they had agreed. (*Moheet.*)

But when the cultivator supplies the seed, it is lawful without such permission.

When a person gives up his land to another to sow it for this year with his own seed, on condition that the crop shall belong to both, in halves, (whether he say or do not say "do with it as you please,") and the cultivator delivers the land with seed to another person in *Moozâraüt* at a half, this is

mal. Indeed, it is expressly stated in the same authority, that a right is not *mal*. *Mal* may be considered, either as specific or as indeterminate. In the former case it is called, in the Moohummudan Law, *ayn*, or a thing, and in the latter *deyn*, or obligation, as it is only through the obligation of some one that things taken indeterminately can be made the subject of legal cognizance. It is not easy to distinguish the right to *ayn*, or a specific thing, from the thing itself, but the right to *deyn*, or an obligation, is easily distinguishable from the obligation itself. The former right is called *jus in re*, by the civilians, and the latter *jus ad rem*. *Ayn* and *Deyn* are both fit objects of transfer, either by sale or gift, according to the Moohummudan Law. So also is the right to *ayn*, or the *jus in re;* but the right to *deyn*, or *jus ad rem*, or, in other words, the power of a creditor to exact the payment or performance of an obligation, is not a proper object of transfer, nor can the benefit to be derived from it be conferred on any other than the debtor himself; as, for instance, by releasing or cancelling the debt. (*Hidayah* and *Kifayah*, vol. iii. p. 615.)

The *Mookasimah Khiraj* is described as a share of an actually existing crop, and is therefore specific or *ayn;* and the *Wuzeefa* is described as an obligation, and is therefore indeterminate, or *deyn*. In both cases it is obviously the things themselves, and not the rights to them, that are intended; and in this sense both the *Mookasimah* and *Wuzeefa Khiraj* are properly described as *mal*, and are fit subjects of transfer. The right to the *Mookasimah* (which being a specific right is scarcely distinguishable from the thing itself) is also transferable; but the right to the *Wuzeefa*, being a right to an obligation, cannot be legally nor even effectually transferred, in any way, known to the Moohummudan Law. What has been said has reference only to the *Khiraj* of the year; for as to the right to the *Khiraj* of future years, which has not yet accrued, it is in both cases a mere naked right, that cannot, in any sense, be said to be the subject of transfer. I am, therefore, inclined to think that what some writers have supposed to be transfers of the right to the *Khiraj*, were, in reality, what they generally appear to be, either transfers of land, or only orders for payment of the *Khiraj*, as it might accrue, in favour of particular individuals. On the subject of things and obligations, see *Moohummudan Law of Sale* (*Baillie*), Introduction.

lawful, and when the produce is obtained, one half will go to that other person in exchange for his labour, as declared to him by the owner of the seed, and half to the owner of the land in exchange for the usufruct of his land, as stipulated with him by the owner of the seed, the owner of the seed himself getting nothing. And if the land had been given up to the first to work it with his seed, on condition that the crop should be between them, in halves, and the first should deliver it to the second to labour it with his seed, on condition that the second should have two-thirds of the produce, and the first one-third, and the second should work it accordingly, he would have two-thirds of the produce; for the produce being an increase from his seed no one can have any right to it, except by special agreement; but as he agreed for a third of the produce to the first, this third will go to the landlord, who will also be entitled, as against the first cultivator, to a hire or rent proportioned to the third of his land. But suppose the seed to be furnished by the first, the second would then have a third of the produce as declared to him by the first cultivator, and the landlord another third, he being also entitled, as against the first, to another third, as the rent of his land. (*Mubsoot.*) A person delivers up his land to another to sow with seed belonging to them both, the cattle to be furnished by the cultivator,[1] on condition that the crop shall be to both in halves, and the cultivator makes a third party partner with him as to his share, and he acts with him accordingly; both the *Moozâraüt* and the partnership are void, and the produce belongs to the two original parties, in proportion to their seed, the owner of the land having further a claim on the first cultivator for the rent of half the land, and the second labourer having also a claim upon him for the hire of his labour, because he worked under an invalid contract of hiring; but the first cultivator has no claim on the landlord for the hire of his labour, because he worked in a matter in which he was a partner, and has no right to hire for it, and the first cultivator is bound to bestow in charity the surplus of his

[1] Arab. *Akkar.* See *ante*, page 19, note 1.

maintenance and of the value of his seed, because it is a surplus which he has derived from the land of another under an invalid lease. (*Futawa Koobra.*)

Sowing lands without a contract.

* A person gives up his land to another in *Moozâraüt*, for a year, that the cultivator may sow it with his own seed; he does so, and then sows it again after the expiration of the year, without the permission of the owner; the owner being informed of what has been done, does not sanction it, (it matters not, whether before or after the springing of the plant); it has been said that if it were the custom in that village,[1] for the people to sow their lands, time after time, without renewing their contracts, this would be lawful, and the produce be divided among the parties, on the same terms as stipulated for in the expired contract. But it is related of Sheikh Ismaeel Al Zahid, that he declared, that this case is mentioned in the book,[2] as being unlawful, and that the cultivator is bound, after deducting an amount sufficient to compensate him for his own labour and that of his cattle, and also for his seed, to apply the remainders in charity, as in a case of usurpation; and that he also declared, our doctors were in the practice of deciding according to the book, but "I have seen in other books that it is lawful, in the same way, as if one should give up his land to a person, and say, 'I have given up this land to you on the same terms as such an one had it the former year,' which would be lawful; and this is also to be preferred. He[3] has said, "and in my opinion, if the land were prepared, or in a fit condition to be given up in *Moozâraüt*, and the share of the labourer in the produce were well known among the people of that village,[4] and there was no difference on the subject, and a person should sow the land, it would be lawful on a liberal construction of the law; but if the land were not prepared or fit to be given up in *Moozâraüt*, or if the share

* N.B. The authorities, from this to the end, are from Chapter xiii. p. 415—416.

1 Arab. *kureeut*.

2 It does not appear what book is referred to.

3 Who does not appear, unless Ismaeel himself is intended.

4 Arab. *Mowza*.

of the labourer in the produce were not known to be one or uniform, but different among the people of that village, (*Mowza*,) it would not be lawful, and the cultivator would be an usurper; regard being had to custom, if the fact of his being an usurper is not ascertained; but if it be known that he sowed the land by usurpation, as for instance, if he had declared at the time of sowing, that he sowed the land for himself, and not in *Moozâraüt*, or if he were a person who does not take land in *Moozâraüt*, being eminent or well known as such, then it would be an act of usurpation, and the crop would belong to him, but he would be responsible for damage to the land. (*Futawa Kazee Khan.*) And I have seen in some *Futwas*, as follows:[1] there are lands in a village,[2] either *wukf* or proprietary, and it is the custom of that village, that whoever it may be, cultivates this land, without asking permission from the superintendent of the *wukf*, and neither proprietors nor the superintendent of proprietors forbid them, but the labourers at the time of the ripening of the corn, give the *Dihkany*[3] share, and do not refuse it. If any one should cultivate such land without taking it in *Moozâraüt* from the owner[4] or superintendent, this sowing of his is to be considered as by way of *Moozâraüt*. But if it be a *mowza* in which they always act with the permission of the owner, and when any one acts without his permission, the owner forbids, or the owner usually acts for himself; then if any one should act without permission of the owner or superintendent, we should treat it as a *Moozâraüt* where the land is *wukf*, but not so where it is proprietary. (*Moheet.*)

[1] The whole of what follows is in Persian.
[2] Persian, *Deeh*.
[3] Tillage. It has other meanings. The share of the owner of the *Dih* or village, seems to be intended.
[4] Persian, *Khoodawind*, lord or master.

APPENDIX.

No. I.

TRANSLATION OF A FIRMAUN, CONCERNING THE COLLECTION OF TRIBUTE, ISSUED BY THE EMPERÓR ALUMGEER (AURUNGZEBE), IN A.H. 1079, OR A.D. 1688.

[Copied from Mr. C. W. Boughton Rouse's *Dissertation concerning the Landed Property of Bengal.*]

To the trusty Mahomed Hashem, whose hope is in the royal favor, be it known. That since by the blessings of the grace and favor of the Lord of the earth and of the heavens, whose benefits are great and universal, it has ever been our desire, so to guide the reins of inclination in our exalted designs, as to conform to the sacred text, which says, "Of a truth the Lord commandeth that you act with justice and with righteousness," so is it our earnest wish in all our arrangements of weight and moment to follow the laws[1] prescribed by the most excellent of created beings[2] (upon whom and upon his posterity, and companions, be the sublimest blessings and peace), and by continually revolving in our enlightened mind, "That the earth and the heavens stand firm through justice," perform our devotions Appendix.

[1] The *Futawa Alumgeeree* must have been completed before the date assigned to this Firmaun, for it was commenced about A.D. 1670.

[2] Moohummud.

Appendix. towards Providence, and venerate His commands, by showing pity and indulgence towards our subjects of every degree.

Wherefore, on the present fortunate occasion, we have caused to be issued this sublime mandate, the emblem of justice, in order that the Mutteseddies and Aumils now in office, as well as those who may be hereafter employed in the affairs of the protected dominions of Hindoostan, from one extremity to the other, be informed in all points concerning the Tribute, as to the quantity and mode directed in the enlightened law of the pure and bright religion. To this edict are subjoined the distinctions which are approved, as being ascertained from good and authentic traditions, and according to which they are to make the collections. They shall not require an annual renovation of this edict; but assure themselves that any deviation therefrom will make them liable both to temporal and eternal punishment.

First. They must shew the ryotts every kind of favor and indulgence, inquire into their circumstances, and endeavour, by wholesome regulations and wise administration, to engage them with hearty good will, to labor towards the increase of agriculture, so that no lands may be neglected that are capable of cultivation.

Second. From the commencement of the year they shall, as far as they are able, acquire information of the circumstances of every husbandman,[1] whether they are employed in cultivation, or have neglected it. Then those who have the ability, they shall excite and encourage to cultivate their lands; and if they require indulgence in any particular instances, let it be granted them. But if, upon examination, it shall be found, that some who have the ability and are assisted with water, nevertheless have neglected to cultivate their lands, they shall admonish and threaten, and use force and stripes In *Kheraj Mowezzef*,[2] they shall acquire in-

[1] "*Moozarea*" is commonly translated "husbandman," and it is probable that it is the original word here. The whole tenor of the passage indicates that the husbandmen are the *Moozarea* of the state, and renders it highly probable that it refers to land of which the state was the proprietor.

[2] See *ante*, page 3, note 6.

formation of the conduct of the proprietors of land from whom this tribute is to be collected, whether they cultivate or not;[1] and if they learn that the husbandmen are unable to provide the implements of husbandry, they shall advance them money from government, in the way of *Tekawy*, and take a security.[2] Appendix.

Third. In *Kheraj Mowezzef*, if the proprietor of the land, for want of means of providing the implements of husbandry, has been unable to cultivate it, or has deserted, leaving the land uncultivated, they shall either give the land in farm, or allow another to cultivate it (on account of the proprietor). In case it is given in farm, they shall take the tribute out of the farm; or if it is cultivated by another, from the proprietor's share,[3] and if any balance remains, cause it to be sent to the proprietor, or they shall appoint a person to succeed the proprietor, who shall cultivate the land; and after paying the tribute, whatever remains, he shall apply to his own use.[4] When the proprietors of the land shall again have the ability to cultivate them, they shall be restored to them.[5] If a person deserts, leaving his land uncultivated, they shall not give it in farm during the remainder of that year, but after the expiration of that year they shall give it in farm.[6]

Fourth. Let them obtain information of the parcels of lands which, having fallen into disuse, have not been restored to cultivation. If they are situated amongst highways and roads, let them be annexed to the (neighbouring[7]) city or town, that somebody may cultivate them. If they are of

[1] See page 13.
[2] This is agreeable to Aboo Yoosuf's opinion, as stated page 15.
[3] Alluding, apparently, to a case where the land is given in *Moozaraut*.
[4] The whole of this is in conformity with the course pointed out in page 14, as proper to be adopted in the case of the proprietor's inability to cultivate.
[5] See page 15, at foot.
[6] This accords with the *Siraj-ool-wuhhaj*, as quoted in page 16.
[7] Where parentheses occur, they seem to have been added by the translator, who was Mr. Gladwin.

Appendix. other descriptions, let them examine the state of such lands. Provided some part is cultivated, but is not very hopeful, they shall not give molestation on account of the tribute of such lands. If there are but small hopes from the remainder (of bringing it back into cultivation), or if it has been all along uncultivated; in both cases, if that land is proprietary, the proprietor being present, and capable of cultivating it, let them admonish him to cultivate it. But if that land is not proprietary, or the proprietor is not known, let them give it to a person who is capable of cultivating it. Then if the farmer is a Mussulman, and the aforesaid land is situated in the neighbourhood of *Asheree* land, let them agree with him for *Asher*. If it lies near *Kherajee* land, or the farmer is an infidel, they shall positively exact from him the *Kheraj*[1] (*Mowezzef.*)[2] In a case where such *Kheraj* is not proper, they shall, according to the exigency of the occasion, settle a rate for each Beegah, which is called *Kheraj Mekettaat*,[3] or else settle for half of the established share of the produce, which is called *Mokossimeh*. If the proprietor is known, but is totally incapable of cultivating the land, provided that land was heretofore settled for *Kheraj Mokossimeh*, let them act conformably to the directions hereinafter given.[4] If it was not *Mokossimeh*, they shall not give any molestation for *Asher*, or for *Kheraj* (*Mowezzef*); but in case of distress, having advanced him Tekawy, they shall make him employ himself in cultivation.

Fifth. If the proprietor of a piece of uncultivated ground be known, let them leave it to him, and not suffer any other to possess it. If the proprietor thereof is not known, and the soil is not promising, they shall, according to the best of

[1] This is agreeable to what is stated in page 3, as founded on the opinions of Aboo Huneefa and Aboo Yoosuf.

[2] The *Wuzeefa* or *Moowuzzuf* is always to be implied where the *Mookasimah* is not particularly mentioned.

[3] The explanation that precedes this word has probably been inserted by the translator; for the literal meaning of the term see page 16, note 2.

[4] No direction after given is applicable to the case, unless what immediately follows is intended.

their judgment, give it to any one they shall think capable of managing it; and if such an one do properly cultivate it, they shall consider him the proprietor. If the land is capable of particular species of cultivation, and he acts in a manner that prevents such a return from the soil (as might, with proper management, be obtained) they shall hinder him from so doing; and they shall prevent him from enjoying the profits thereof, nor allow any person to possess such land, or to be considered as the proprietor.[1] Appendix.

If a piece of ground has changed its proprietor, and through his (the new proprietor's) mismanagement become entirely desolate, they shall consider it as belonging to him who possessed it before, and not allow this other to possess it.

Sixth. In a place where neither *Asher* nor *Kheraj* (*Mowezzef*) are yet settled upon agriculture, they shall act as directed in the law.[2] In a case of *Kheraj* (*Mowezzef*) they shall settle for such a rate that the ryots may not be ruined by the lands; and they shall not on any account exact beyond (the value of) half of the produce, notwithstanding any (particular) ability to pay more.[3] In a place where (one or the other) is fixed, they shall take what has been agreed for, provided that in *Kheraj* (*Mowezzef*) it does not exceed half (of the produce in money) that the Ryots may not be ruined. But if (what is settled appears to be too much) they shall reduce the former *Kheraj* to what shall be found proportionate to their ability; however, if the capacity exceeds the settlement, they shall not take more.[4]

Seventh. Commutations of *Mowezzef* and *Mokossimeh* are allowable, provided the ryots are satisfied, but otherwise they shall not make such alterations.[5]

[1] The whole of this paragraph relates to waste land, which cannot be cultivated without the permission of the Imam, whom the Sooltan is supposed to represent. See page 42.

[2] That is, they will fix either *Ooshr* or *Khiraj* upon the lands as may be agreeable to the general principles of the law.

[3] It appears from this that they were at liberty to fix a *Wuzeefa* or *Mookassimah Khiraj* as they might think proper, but whatever it might be, it was not in any case to exceed the extreme limit of the *Mookassimah*.

[4] See page 6. [5] See page 7.

Appendix. Eight. The season for demanding the *Kheraj Mowezzef* on every species is, when the harvest is fit for reaping;[1] therefore, from every particular species that shall arrive at that state, they shall take the proportion of tribute.[2]

Ninth. When a field that pays *Kheraj Mowezzef*, suffers a partial injury, they shall make a careful investigation thereof, and shall allow a fair and equitable deduction, according to the degree of injury,[3] and in taking the tribute from the remainder, they shall do it in such manner, that the ryots may enjoy a complete half (of what the crop ought to have produced).

Tenth. In *Kheraj Mowezzef*. Whosoever, notwithstanding he possesses the ability to cultivate his own land, and meets with no impediment, nevertheless suffers it to be uncultivated; let them exact the tribute from other means. If in particular cases, from inundation, or from want of rain before the reaping of the harvest, it suffers such a degree of injury that the seed thereof doth not come to his hand, and there remain not sufficient time for him to cultivate again that year, they shall consider the tribute to have ceased. But if the injury shall happen after the reaping, even if there be a total loss, such as having been eaten by cattle, &c., or if there remain sufficient time for a second cultivation (in that year) they shall exact the tribute.[4]

Eleventh. If the proprietor of land paying *Mowezzef* cultivates it himself, and dies before he had paid the tribute of that year, and the harvest comes to the hands of his heirs, they shall exact the tribute from the heirs.[5] If the aforesaid defunct died before he had cultivated the land, and there was not remaining sufficient time for cultivating it in that year, they shall not exact anything.

Twelfth. In *Mowezzef*. If the proprietor gives his own ground in farm, or lends it to another, and the farmer or

[1] Though the proprietor becomes liable at the beginning of the year, according to Aboo Huneefa (page 21), it does not follow that the debt is then payable; on the contrary, to exact it then would be taking it in advance, and mere oppresssion. (*Ante*, page 10.)

[2] See page 21. [3] Page 6.

[4] See page 18. [5] Page 21, note 2.

borrower cultivates it, the tribute shall be exacted from the proprietor.[1] If either of them makes a garden on it, they shall demand the tribute from the farmer or the borrower. If any one takes possession of (such) tributary land, and denies having done so, provided the proprietor has witnesses, and the usuper has cultivated the ground, they shall exact the tribute from the usurper; but if he has not cultivated it, they shall not exact the tribute from either. If the usurper denies the fact, and the proprietor cannot produce witnesses, they shall exact the tribute from the proprietor. In a case of mortgage, they shall act the same as directed concerning an usurper; provided the mortgagee has cultivated the land without the permission of the mortgager.[2] Appendix.

Thirteenth. In *Kheraj Mowezzef.* If a person sells part of his own such tributary land, which is arable, and produces only one crop (in the year), provided there remains sufficient time to cultivate in that year, and the buyer has taken possession, (seeing that) if he wishes to cultivate in that year, nobody can hinder him, therefore the tribute shall be exacted from him, but otherwise it shall be taken from the seller. If it produces two crops (in one year) one of which has been enjoyed by the seller, and the other by the buyer, the tribute shall be equally divided between them. If on that land there is a crop fit for reaping, the tribute shall be taken from the seller.[3]

Fourteenth. In *Mowezzef.* If any person builds a house upon his own ground (which was cultivated) he shall pay the same tribute that he paid before; and the same if he has planted trees that do not produce fruit. If a cultivated spot, that paid the *Kheraj Mowezzef* is converted into a garden, and the whole closely planted with fruit tress, they shall exact 2¾ rupees, being the rate for a garden,[4] although the

[1] Conformable to page 8.

[2] All this is in exact conformity with what is stated in page 8.

[3] See page 9.

[4] Compare with page 20. As the rate for a garden was 10 *dirhems*, this shews that in the time of Aurungzebe 10 *dirhems* were equal to 2¾ rupees, which would give only 4⅖ths anas for the value of a *dirhem*.

Appendix. tress have not yielded fruit, excepting upon vines and almond tress, whereon tribute is not due until they bear fruit; but when they produce fruit, they shall exact from them 2¾ rupees, upon the supposition that a lawful Beegah, measuring 45 Shahjehany or 60 lawful Guz, square, will yield 5½ rupees, but otherwise they shall take half of the actual produce. If the value of the produce is less than a fourth of a rupee, in the proportion of one seer out of five Shahjehany seers of grain, they shall not take it according to such deficiency.[1]

If an infidel sells his land to a Mussulman, notwithstanding his being a Mussulman, they shall exact from him *Kheraj*[2] (*Mowezzef*).

Fifteenth. If any one dedicates his own land to the use of a public burying-ground, or for a *serai*, they shall consider the tribute to have ceased.

Sixteenth. In Kheraj Mokossimeh. Every one who is not the (hereditary) proprietor of such Kheraj land, whether infidel or Mussulman, having bought it, or taken it in mortgage, shall receive the profits with permission (of government). From whatever is produced on that land they shall exact the settled rate of tribute, provided it be not more than half (of the produce), in which case they shall reduce it; but if it is less than the third, they shall increase it as far as they may deem fit.

Seventeenth. If the proprietor of Mokossimeh land dies, and leaves not any heirs; in giving that land in farm, or to be cultivated, &c., they shall act in the manner already directed under the head of Mowezzef.

Eighteenth. In Mokossimeh. If an injury happens to the harvest, upon as much as is damaged, they shall not exact the tribute, and whether the injury happens to the grain before or after reaping, they shall exact the tribute from (only) what remains (good).[3]

[1] So in the copy, but I do not understand what it means.

[2] Page 7.

[3] See *ante*, page 19.

No. II.

FIRMAN FOR THE APPOINTMENT OF A JAGEER.[1]

[This and the remaining numbers of the Appendix are copied from Dr. Francis Balfour's translation of THE FORMS OF HERKERN. The Originals are in Persian.]

At this time the mandate of high dignity hath obtained the honor of manifestation, viz. that, in consequence of the removal of the flower of great noblemen Mirza Feridoon, I have confirmed, by way of Jageer, from the beginning of the season of Autumn, the sum of twenty-one lacks of dams,[2] out of the Purgunneh of Khizrabad, as it is specified on the back of the Firman, to the approved in service, the attendant of our imperial presence, Nadir Khan. It is required that the Chowdries, Kanongoes, Muckuddims, and peasantry of the said Pergunneh, having acknowledged the person above named Jageerdar of that place, and having given an account of the just rent,[3] and of the duties of Diwani, according to the established agreement, to the agents of the said Khan, shall in no respect occasion any diminution or deduction; and whatever the former Jageerdar shall have collected from the said crop, having taken it back, let them give it to to him; considering this as peremptory, and having acted according to royal command, let them deliver it up. Appendix.

[1] This word is compounded of two Persian words, viz. *ja* (place) and *geer* (take,) imperative of the verb *Girifteen* to seize, but here taken for the participle *Geerindu*, seizer or taker. The combination means properly *place taker*, but it is commonly used as a substantive noun, and hence irregularly construed with the word *Dar*, or holder, as *Jageerdar*.

[2] According to the Ayeen Akbery there are 40 dams in a rupee; and the sum would therefore be Rs. 52,500 or about £5,250.

[3] *Mal Wajibee;* Arabic words that signify literally "property due or necessary," but here evidently applied to the revenue or *Khiraj*. See *ante*, page 65, note.

No. III.

PERWANNEH[1] FOR HOLDING A JAGEER.

Appendix. Whereas, according to the world-subjecting sun-resplendent mandate, the sum of five lacks of dams, in the Pergunneh of Feridabad, in consequence of the removal of the noble and princely Mozuffer Khan, having been bestowed and conferred on the illustrious and noble Behader Khan, by way of Jageer, from the commencement of the season of Autumn; and a second time represented on the 21st of Jummadissani, the *Sabti*[2] is now drawing out a royal commission for this purpose, it is required that the Chowdries, Kanoongoes, and husbandry of the said Pergunneh, having acknowledged the said person Jageerdar of that place, shall give an account of the just rent and dues of the Dewani, to the agent of the said Khan, and shall not withhold or deduct a single dam from that sum. And whatever the former Jageerdar shall have collected, after deducting the dues of collection, let it be returned to the agent of the present Jageerdar, considering this as peremptory, let them act according to instructions.

[1] The Firman may be said to constitute the *Jageer*. The Perwanneh is a requisition addressed to the officers of the Pergunneh to recognize the person appointed as Jageerdar, so that there are properly a Firman and Perwanneh for each *Jageer*, though this Perwanneh happens to relate to a different appointment than is contained in the preceding Firman.

[2] A person whose duty is to make out Commissions. (*Balfour*.)

No. IV.

PERWANNEH TO A JAGEERDAR ON THE SUBJECT OF A COMPLAINT.

It is signified to the agent of the Jageerdar of the Pergunneh of Goheram, that at this time Gunher Saho has come and complained that he has a demand on Dowlet Khan, the Afghan (for a sum borrowed upon bond), who is dilatory and obstinate in the payment of it; it is required that if this be the case, they will cause him to pay whatever is due; that he who is in the right may receive justice. And if it be otherwise, let him submit the affair to the decision of the noble law; that violence may not be allowed. Let him consider this as positive. Appendix.

No. V.

FIRMAN FOR A MAINTENANCE.[1]

Appendix. At this time the fortunate and auspicious edict has obtained the honor of proclamation, and the dignity of publication, viz. that I have granted the extent of 300 Begas of land, half sowed, half fallow, out of the Pergunneh of Illahidadpoor of the district of Kinnowj, by way of maintenance for the reverend and excellent, the perfect and pure shaikh Abdulghufar, and his posterity,[2] from the season of autumn: that having applied its revenues to his own use, season after season, and year after year, he may dedicate his study and attention to praying for the continuance of our daily increasing prosperity. It is required that the superiors and managers of that Pergunneh having measured and marked out the said land in a good situation, shall leave it at the disposal of the person above mentioned. After the boundaries are ascertained, let them not encroach upon it. And on account of rent and duties, such as Kunurra, Paishkush, measurement money, and fees of entry, and all the extortions[3] of the Dewany, and demands of government, let them occasion him no trouble. And having considered him as free, and exempted from all kinds of taxation, let them not require every year a fresh Firman or Perwaneh. Having acted according to command, let them make no resistance.

[1] *Mudud maash;* a compound of two Arabic words, which signify assistance and living.

[2] *Furzundan*, plural of *Furzund*, child. It has a technical meaning, which is given in the Introduction.

[3] This word is curious, as occurring in a royal Firman. It is, perhaps, a little too strong for the original, which means, literally, vexations or troubles.

No. VI.

PERWANNEH FOR A MAINTENANCE.

Let the Muttissuddies of important affairs for the present and future, of the Pergunneh of Fereedabad know, that whereas, agreeable to our auspicious mandate, the extent of an hundred and fifty Beegahs of land, half cultivated and half fallow, is given by way of maintenance out of the said Pergunneh, from the beginning of the autumnal season, to the reverend and learned Abdirreheem;[1] it is required that, agreeable to the order, having measured and marked out the said land in a good spot, they shall put it into the aforesaid's possession; that having, every season, appropriated the revenue of it to his own use, he may be employed in prayer for our daily increasing prosperity. And on account of rent and expences, let them by no manner of means give him any trouble. And let them not every year require a renewal of his Firman and Perwanneh. Let them consider this as positive, and act as directed. Appendix.

[1] It will be observed that there is no allusion to posterity here.

No. VII.

FIRMAN FOR A PREFERMENT AND REMOVAL.

Appendix. As the attention of our august soul is dedicated to the tranquillity of the state, and to the management of the affairs of our old servants who have spent their precious lives in labour and attachment, with perfect honesty and fidelity; on this account, the ancient in service, the cream of our sincere well-wishers, the pattern of our servants, devoted from attachment, Khajeh Ibraheem, who was long ago appointed to the respectable office of paymaster to our successful army, and has at no time polluted the mantle of his inclination with the dust of embezzlement or neglect; and performed the duties of that office according to the pleasure of our most pure and princely soul; as the frailty of mortality and infirmity has now overcome him, regarding the length of his service, and natural attachment, and out of our royal indulgence excusing him from duty, we have given him by way of perpetual gift the sum of five lacks of dams out of the Pergunneh of Beherampoor, his usual abode, in compliance with his own request; that having dedicated that sum season after season, and year after year, to his own use, he may employ his diligence and attention in praying for our eternal prosperity. It is required that the officers and agents and Jageerdars, both now and hereafter, having acted according to our sacred command, and having measured and marked out the land for the sum specified, in a good place, shall put it into the aforesaid's possession. And having considered him as free and exempted from every taxation and all public burdens, let them in no respect give his agents any trouble. With regard to the Chowdhries, Kanoongoes, Muckuddims, and farmers of tha place, let them account for the lawful rent and dues of the Dewanny to the agent of that old servant; and let them occasion no diminution or deduction; and let them not deviate from his commands.

INDEX

ARABIC AND PERSIAN TERMS.

www.ingramcontent.com/pod-product-compliance
Lightning Source LLC
Chambersburg PA
CBHW061355240926
51846CB00007B/1418
9789366086866